The Preparation for the Coming of the Messiah

Part 1 of 3

The messages spoken from 1970 to 1973 by the spiritual messengers of God, Aka, on the coming of the Messiah

This book is dedicated to God in gratitude for sending
His spiritual messengers to Earth
to prepare a way for the coming of the Messiah.

And it is dedicated to all people who will prepare
a place within their hearts for his coming.

Hark! For those who have ears to hear let them hear.
And for those who have eyes to see let them see.

"We are here but for one purpose, and that is to prepare the way for the coming of the Messiah"

Almost 2,000 years ago, Jesus said, "I will pray the Father, and He will give you another Helper, that He may abide with you forever — the Spirit of truth, whom the world cannot receive, because it neither sees Him nor knows Him; but you know Him, for He dwells with you and will be in you. I will not leave you orphans; I will come to you." (*John* 14:16–18)

Jesus gave this loving promise at his last Passover supper on April 1, AD 33, the gospel of *John* reveals. The gospels of *Matthew, Mark*, and *Luke* say the traditional Passover was Thursday, April 2. The U.S. Naval Observatory calculates that April 3 was the day that Jesus said this because of a planetary alignment and an earthquake in Israel.

What we do know is 1,936 years later, while the world was celebrating the Christ-child's birth, a new comet was discovered by a South African astronomer Christmas week, on December 28, 1969. It came as a sign from God of a gift He would soon be giving to Earth, to all who wish to receive.

As the heavenly light grew brighter and brighter, it passed over Earth, March 26, 1970. In early April, its radiance shone for all the world to see.

God has sent His spiritual messengers again to Earth, in answer to Jesus' prayer. They began to speak to us — and to the world — from a town called, Globe, through an unconscious man (Ray Elkins). We first recorded their voice on April 3, 1970.

The shepherds in the fields tending their flocks at night surely would have done so too. Their account of that holy night is written in *Luke*, chapter 2:

"And behold, an angel of the Lord stood before them, and the glory of the Lord shone around them, and they were greatly afraid.

Then the angel said to them, 'Do not be afraid, for behold, I bring you good tidings of great joy which will be to all people'....

And suddenly there was with the angel a multitude of the heavenly host praising God and saying: 'Glory to God in the highest; and on earth peace, good will toward men!'"

On a night so silent no one heard was a glorious coming!

On Christmas week in 1969, as the birth of Christ was celebrated and the Second Coming awaited, the light was first seen.

The light grew brighter and brighter, shining in the heavens so radiantly as it passed over Earth before early April, the time when Jesus had made his Passover promise, died and was resurrected. At that time, in 1970, a man named Ray Elkins passed on. "One with more love in his eyes than anyone" he had ever seen gave him a gift, and the choice to remain there with all the others who were gathered around this one seated in their midst, or to return to his body. If Ray returned, he was asked to give this gift to others in the same manner of love it was given to him, freely, asking nothing in return. Ray didn't know what the gift was. He only saw the great love in those eyes, and choose to return.

Soon after he returned, this gift began to speak through the unconscious man — in a voice we could hear and understand.

The heavenly light shone brightly throughout April and May 1970, the same months when Jesus died and was resurrected, and then spoke to his disciples.

In early April, at his last Passover supper, Jesus had said: "But now I go away to Him who sent Me, and none of you asks Me, 'Where are You going?' But because I have said these things to you, sorrow has filled your heart. Nevertheless I tell you the truth. It is to your advantage that I go away; for if I do not go away, the Helper will not come to you; but if I depart, I will send Him to you. *(John* 16:5–7)

Jesus prayed "for those who will believe in Me through their word; that they all may be one, as You, Father, *are* in Me, and I in You; that they also may be one in Us, that the world may believe that You sent Me. And the glory which You gave Me I have given them, that they may be one just as We are one: I in them, and You in Me; that they may be made perfect in one, and that the world may know that You have sent Me, and have loved them as You have loved Me." (*John* 17:20–24)

Near Christmas, 1969, a new comet was discovered, which grew brighter until the time Aka, the spiritual messengers of God, came as it passed closest over Earth, March 26, 1970, the day many were remembering Jesus farewell words and his promise to return. As the light shone brightly overhead, a voice began to speak through Ray's unconscious body. As it shone throughout April and in May, some thought it was the most spectacular heavenly light of the century. **"You ask if this new comet were part of our coming, and I shall say, yes, for there was a sign in the sky for the enlightenment of man's soul,"** *the spiritual messengers of God, Aka, answered on April 13, 1970. On May 21, 1970, the spiritual messengers of God said:* **For now, as we have told soul Ray — now shall be the time of the Cherub. It shall burn brightly in thy heavens for all to see. Look thee toward the east from which we come, and ye shall see. This shall be proof to mankind of our coming.**

From April 3, 1970 through the next 19 years, the voice spoke in such love—giving guidance, healing, teachings, parables, and prophecies.

Three months after the spiritual messengers of God arrived on Earth, they said on July 15, 1970: Now, thy would ask again of us, who comes to you, and from where we came?

For we were sent for one who asked God.

And he who sent [us] and asks did say, "Father, send Thy these who would teach, and send Thy these who would know of my Father." There were those before him who did the same....[See *John* 13:14-17, 20; 14:1-5, 15-21, 27-29; John 16:16-19,22-24, *The Revelation of John* 5:1-7.]

We have made ourselves known to you as our Father has suggested.

For we call, as thy would call it, ourselves, Aka. Think thee of the first of the name, Aka, and thy will think of the Almighty. Think of the second of the name, and thy will think of the word, karmic. Think of the last of the name, and thy will think of the records, the records which are kept from the beginning, of all planes, of all knowledge, which man was born and born again. This knowledge, as our Father gives us permission, we should give of thee. We give this knowledge so that man, all of man, would know the love of our Father. And by knowing of the love our Father has to give, of the tears our Father sheds, that all man, of all religions, should come to our Father together in peace and love.

September 24, 1971: And as we have said before, we are not great. We are here for but one purpose, to prepare the way for the coming of the Messiah — and that he may walk upon holy ground.

Then we should say unto thee these words. Blessed are they who should worship unto our Father. Blessed are they who should give unto the poor. And blessed are they who should give glory unto our Father this day.

For hark, we should say unto thee these words. For [He] should give unto thee a new Book upon this day....

But we should say unto thee these words. As a woman should give birth unto a child, so should our Lord give birth unto your minds.

And as the pain is great before the birth, but therefore, upon the birth and the knowledge of new birth upon thy earth, this should give thee great joy, and therefore, thy should forget of the pain that came before the birth. [See *John* 16:18–24.]

Therefore, our Father should place great joy upon thy minds.

It matters [not, of naught] to our Father that thy should climb His ladder slowly. But what does matter to our Father is your struggles to climb it at all. And therefore, should you give glory unto our Father, our Father, therefore, gives glory unto His children.

And we should say unto thee these words. Was not the one known as Jesus Christ, did not God prefer that he be born upon your earth...Your Father did bring upon your earth His firstborn child, therefore, to show unto His children the truth of our Father's Law, and to fulfill the prophecies of the prophets.

And therefore, once again these prophecies shall be fulfilled upon thy earth.

And we should say unto thee these words. We have much knowledge; we have many messages that we should give unto thee from our Father. Be patient, for as good wine should take time to make, so should the knowledge of God in the telling take time.

Editor's note: We were able to tape record what the spiritual messengers of God spoke through their unconscious instrument, Ray Elkins of Globe, Arizona, from 1970 through 1989. Their words were transcribed. In this writing, their messages found in a search for the phrase, "coming of the Messiah," are gathered for you to read.

*Their words are unedited, and simply placed in order by the date they were spoken. The angels' messages are in bold font to help the reader know who is speaking. After you read this Part 1 of 3 of **The Preparation for the Coming of the Messiah**, you may want to read Part 2 of 3 of their messages on the "coming of the Messiah" that they spoke from 1974 to 1977 and then Part 3 of 3, spoken from 1978 to 1989.*

The 1970 messages on the Coming

On June 6, 1970, the spiritual messengers of God, Aka, said: As I have spoke of the birth of a child, the birth of the return of the Messiah of earth — a child shall be born, for he shall lead the souls of the earth plane, as he shall lead the souls of our plane.

And as I have said before, and I say "not as I, but as we," for we are here to prepare a way for his coming.

If our coming is successful, then all shall be in readiness and God's plan shall be told to thee in completion. Now — now shall be the time of the Cherub.

June 16, 1970: As Matthew walked with Christ and asked not for favor, think thee not as Judas who gained but silver, for in thy heart thy know that the material things that are necessary for thy family are already here. So, for what thy would seek is the same thing that Jesus gave to Matthew, and that is all around you, for that is God's work.

There are many times that God has shed teardrops for His children, not only on your world, but upon many worlds. And that this world shall overcome its karma and that God's work shall be complete –

For, as we have said before, we are not great, we are but messengers of God, and we are here to prepare a way. For there shall be a thousand years of peace upon thy earth, but not as thy would count, but as God would count.

And the time grows near that the Messiah shall be known to thee; therefore, sometimes we should be, or seem to be, impatient for our search for souls.

July 1, 1970: Now, we would tell you of a time which was before, when most men, with hate and greed, destroyed the things they loved most, a time of Atlantis. And by telling you of this time, you will know what can happen again; for all the knowledge that came to them was buried beneath the earth, there to remain.

As we have said before, this knowledge is — soon — all parts of it, shall rise again. What was dark shall be lighted; what was buried shall be uncovered, for as we have said before, now is the time of the Cherub —

for we are here to prepare a way — for we seek a place that the Messiah may enter. The time that he shall be known to you grows close.

Therefore, our time grows smaller.

If thy would look at the last words that Christ, Jesus, said before he left his physical body, then, to return to it, you will understand of what we speak of.

July 3, 1970: Now, we would say to thee, for your other answers, look into thy self, and ask again. But do it in this way. For two days, think as thy would go to sleep at night, first of God, then of us, that we might come to you. And we shall, if you want this. If thy do not want it, then this we cannot do. For permission always must be given, both from [thee] and from God. Now can thy understand this?

"I think so. May I ask a question, Aka?"

Yes.

"Was I just now listening to Edgar Cayce, just previously?" Rod asked, about something else that was spoken earlier.

You ask now as a child. But we would answer your question, but permission must be given. If thy would wait, one moment, please.

Yes, permission has been given.

Yes, you were listening, as you would call it, to Edgar Cayce. For now, he is with God. He shall return again on this world at a different time of his own choosing, for then, again, the world shall need him. He shall return — not precisely on the day he thought, but he shall return at the time when the Messiah returns — and therefore, he shall sit in council. Can thy understand this?

"Yes."...

Edgar Cayce was called "the sleeping prophet."
He was known for reading the Akashic records. This photo was taken in 1910.

You have had the thought, why should we, would we choose disciples? We chose them that they may choose souls like yourself to be disciples and disciples again. It is not because each of them are so important; it is because in their minds, from which they came, they have done this work before. Therefore, when we ask them to do it again, and they find this in their soul, they may help to give it to others.

If thy would help but one soul to grasp this.

This thy must understand — we are here for God's work. In doing God's work we are here to prepare a way.

This way is a war of the minds, for the Messiah — for when he is made known — may reign for a thousand years, and we speak of a thousand years, not as you would count them, but as God would count them....

Now, during this time, as we say, that the Messiah shall reign, all those without the body, the soul and the spirit will not enter at this time. Their entries shall not be again until God has completed this part of God's plan. Can thy understand this?

July 20, 1970: Now, now, we should tell thee of the Anti-Christ.

As thy have known and been told before that the time of the Messiah is very near, that we are here to prepare a way — and as the birth shall happen and has happened, then we would tell thee of also, at the same time as the birth of the Messiah, of the birth of the Anti-Christ.

The Anti-Christ shall wear seven crowns, and shall rule seven nations. But we would say of this,

that the Lord, God, our Father, shall protect His children.

Those who would worship the Beast, or the Anti-Christ, which would come from Lucifer, many foul things shall come from its mouth, and it should use thy Lord, our Father, in vain. And it should mock both man and beast, for it knows that its time is short. But fear not, for its rule shall be lean. And God's anger shall be mighty.

As we have told you before, our Lord, God, Father, has taken the necessary steps to protect the Messiah and has taken His protection to the womb of all heaven, and as we have said before,

"on heaven so shall it be on earth."

The war has been fought in two places, and the war shall be won in two places.

But this thy must realize, that now that Satan has been thrown to the earth, and now we would tell thee, for those who have ears to hear, the name of the Anti-Christ shall be six times sixty six — and there shall be the name.

Now, of the Messiah — the Messiah has been transferred unto a place in the desert where our Father shall protect him, and then the Eagle shall spread its wings and shall take this child and protect it, and it shall be protected in the desert. All necessary steps shall be taken that no harm should come to this one.

For when the time of our Lord shall be as one, the Messiah shall rule on the earth as in heaven, and on the earth and many earths across our vast universes.

Now there shall be stars cast from the heavens. And as these stars are cast, so shall Lucifer be chained. [See *The Revelation*, chapters 12, 13, and 19.]

We know thy do not understand of which we speak at this time. But thy soon shall know. Thy shall know of all things, for our Father has opened His mighty door and the light shall shine through for thee to see. Can thy understand of which we speak?

"I think so."

Nay, not at this time thy do not, but soon thy shall.

July 9, 1970: But remember, do *not* misinterpret our words, for by misinterpreting our words, and twisting them to meet thy own ends, thy are creating a new karma. Take of these as they should mean to you, in thy heart and thy soul. Do not add from or take away from any of this.

> *For we, as we have said before, are here to prepare a way for the Messiah, that he may enter into thy world. And as he enters on this earth, so shall it be in heaven. For at that time it shall become God's time.*

And remember this — our Lord shall have the last word in all things.

As was said in the introduction, the spiritual messengers of God answered July 15, 1970: Now, thy would ask again of us, who comes to you, and from where we came? For we were sent for one who asked God. And he who sent [us] and asks did say, "Father, send Thy these who would teach, and send Thy these who would know of my Father." [See *John* 13:14–17, 20; 14:1–5, 15–21, 27–29; John 16:16–19,22–24, *The Revelation of John* 5:1–7.]

There were those before him who did the same....

We have made ourselves known to you as our Father has suggested. For we call, as thy would call it, ourselves, "Aka."

Think thee of the first of the name, Aka, and thy will think of the Almighty. Think of the second of the name, and thy will think of the word, karmic. Think of the last of the name, and thy will think of the records, the records which are kept from the beginning, of all planes, of all knowledge, which man was born and born again. This knowledge, as our Father gives us permission, we should give of thee.

We give this knowledge so that man, all of man, would know the love of our Father. And by knowing of the love our Father has to give, of the tears our Father sheds, that all man, of all religions, should come to our Father together in peace and love.

For we have said before, when thy pray, pray for guidance. This, in itself, is the ending of a karma. Pray for acceptance of thy brothers and thy sisters....

Can thy understand of what we tell thee?...

Then, it does not matter how you spell of this. But if all of you here could agree upon this one simple thing, then you have taken one step closer to our Father.

August 10, 1970: Now, as we have said before, the time of the Cherub is now. Therefore, first we should tell thee, as thy have known before, of our Father, and our Father's plan.

That all may come in accord, we would tell thee that the time of the Messiah is close at hand.

August 24, 1970: Remember, we are here to prepare a way for the Messiah. And as, as those before were called Essene, they were known as those of the time of waiting. We have called this group the philosophy, the Spiritual Philosophy of God.

Now there are others groups, as thy would know them. One of these groups are known as the A.R.E. group. Very soon they shall become part of this work. And this, at this time, we shall say, is good....

Remember, soul John, our Father loves you. If thy could think of us that we may enter, these things shall be put into righteousness again. We have sent many messages, soul John. Prepare thyself, for as we have said before, we are here to prepare a way for the Messiah, and did he not say unto you that you would be here when he arrived, that you would wait upon him?...

We find in this soul [Paul], thy are thinking of, as you would say, a mosaic. This has also entered upon thy wife's mind. Then, we would say, think of the Almighty; think of the records that are kept forever and ever; and, think of the coming of the Messiah. If you may put in thy minds a picture, this would bring all in accord with God.

September 5, 1970 (afternoon): If thy should walk with His hand in yours, then happiness and love for all on your earth plane shall dwell for a thousand years. But remember, those thousand years shall not be as your count; they shall be as our Father counts.

Now, as we have said before,

we are here to prepare a way for the coming of the Messiah; therefore, we, in ourselves, are not important. We are important to God.

Our message, should it be heeded, shall save your earth, as thy would know it.

But remember, our Father made all things, both of the heaven and earth. And those things that belong on the earth shall stay on the earth, and those things that belong in heaven shall stay in heaven. But remember, your earth is only one of many, and your people are only one of many.

Then we say unto you, do not kill this Prophet who comes after us, for if you should try, then God's wrath shall be upon you, and thee shall dwell in a hell, as thy would think it, far beyond anything in thy wildest imagination, for our Father and we shall protect this one.

But now, remember also, at this time shall come the Anti-Christ, and his stay upon your earth shall be lean, and he shall try and stamp upon the foreheads of God's children his name.

Those who may resist this shall stay in the Book which was written in the beginning of time. [*Exodus* 24:1–8. 25:10–22, 26:1–31, 31:1–18, 32:25–34, 33:5–23, 34:1–11, 29, 35:1–19, 37:1–19, 38:21, 39:30–43, 40:1–35, *2 Samuel* 22:7–16, *Ezekiel* 21:11–16, 40:1–4, 41:13–26, 43:1–7, and *The Revelation*, chapters 4–7, 13:11–18, 15:2–4, 17:7–8, 19:1–16, and chapters 20–22.]

And for those who think they have lost their soul, remember, God has set no rules for the worshiping of Him; man has made those rules. God asks only that you love of Him and love of thy brothers and sisters of this earth plane.

September 5, 1970 (evening): Think thee long and hard upon the words you should speak unto others.

Ask that in your meditation that we may enter and we should come unto your mind, for as we have said before that as the spirits of God should flow as a brook, as the souls of man should flow as a river, as the soul of man should flow as an ocean, yet the spirit of man should flow through all.

Yet not all of mankind that walks upon your earth should have of the spiritual form.

Therefore, we should reach you into the many lands. And as you should be reached, so should others, so should be the other knowledge that can be given.

There are many of your kind in the land on which you dwell.

We are here but for one purpose and that purpose is to prepare the way for the coming of the Messiah, and therefore, should build an army of minds. But first, the way must be prepared within yourselves.

Pick your time each day for meditation, quite simply. Then pray unto God that the words of Aka may enter. Therefore, by opening the door we shall enter and make ourselves known unto you. If thy should take of the wine, we should provide of the bread and the yeast, and therefore, thy cup should runneth over. We should await thy answer unto the same.

September 18, 1970:

Open thy mind and thy heart unto us. And as we speak of us, we speak always of our Father first, for remember, we are only the messengers.

We are not important. But if you should think upon the word of Aka, placing the word of God first, we may come into thy mind and give thee, as thy would know them, teaching lessons. In thy meditation, if thy would think upon us, we should send messages. And these messages shall be of five unto you, as they shall be unto all disciples who have been chosen.

But come, soul James, there is much to learn; there is much to prepare for the coming of the Messiah, for this is our reason for being, and yours, but learn of all of this work. But before you teach it, learn of it.

September 25, 1970: Now you ask unto us, "What shall take place between now and this time of a thousand years?"

And we should tell unto you, first, of your famine; this man shall bring upon himself.

The changing of your world, this is part of God's plan, so that all man, of God's people, of God's children, shall become [all] one. Yet, you shall still remain as individuals, with individual thought, individual desire and individual need of food.

This time shall come about as your religions realize that each person has the right to worship his Father in his own way. Our Father intended this; this is why we have said before, "of His many mansions...."

October 5, 1970: *"Aka, at this time, could you give us any more information as to the storing of food and our storing of water?"*

At this time in which thy should ask, we have said unto you, store of the seed, store of the dry fruits or vegetables. Store in such a way that thy may replant and re-grow, and

replenish your earth. Remember, this time we prepare you for is a time that man shall make, not our Father.

The time we prepare you for in the time of one, in the time of the Messiah, this is the time of our Father. For this time, all you shall need shall be furnished you.

But for the time of the Beast, prepare for this time. The time shall be lean, a few months. And this time shall be known in your time as four years, six months. During this time, you should be prepared to provide for yourselves.

We would suggest, for your seed, prepare a place in the ground which is both dark and dry. We should say the same for thy food; prepare a place that is both dark and dry.

Now, we should say unto the water. We have told unto thee the fashions of purifying your water. Now we should tell unto thee, keep ten 1,000-gallon containers in storage. But do not do this until we tell of you. And as we tell of you this, then do it at once, for the water on your earth for a short time shall be foul, and no man, beast or animal, or the bird, or the fowl, or even that of the sea shall be able to drink of this.

October 9, 1970: And now we say unto thee, be transformed.

And we say this into all, as we have said before, the first shall be last and the last shall be first. And upon your heaven shall be your earth, for as all is transformed into five upon your earth, therefore, you shall have a heaven on earth.

And you say unto us, "How could this be possible?" Then we would say unto thee, the time shall come, and this time shall be the time of One, and in this time all man shall be of five, for as it is written, man was made "of our kind, of our likeness." Therefore, your time is near that what thee would know as the God of man and the man-God, for as you were made in "our kind, of our likeness," your power and the power bestowed into man was not equal unto God, but of His likeness. We have said before, should thee choose to walk on the water with us — one moment, please. [See *Genesis* 1:27–28, 5:1–24.]

Our Father — our Father would say these words unto thee.

"AS OF THE TIMES OF [TREPATAN] WHEN MAN'S MINDS COULD WORK AT THEIR FULL CAPACITY, SO IT SHOULD BE AGAIN."

And this time, our Father should have the blood of the Lamb upon your land, for your Messiah shall walk with thee, in every corner of your earth and in every corner of your mind. Then, be ye transformed into our kind, into our likeness.

Can you understand of which we speak?

"No, Aka."

Nay, then unto all disciples shall be these messages. First, our messages and our healing shall come into thy minds, as we have said before, as raindrops.

Now thy enter the storm, and we see the necessity that thy minds shall develop far beyond your wildest imagination. Therefore, we should send these teaching dreams into thee....

Remember, now is the time again of waiting. Now is the time thy shall wait, for this time shall be even more important than was before. For as the Messiah was born before, he shall be born again. Have patience, have faith.

October 23, 1970: *"Aka, we have one question this evening that is the concern, I think, of most of the group. We'd like to ask if you have any information you can give us on the 20- month old, unborn child in Indonesia?"*

You shall find, as we have spoke before, that as a stone is cast into the brook that would flow to the rivers, that should flow to the ocean, and therefore, flow to the many nations, new leaders in all of the nations shall be needed. These leaders shall be mighty men and women. And they should give unto your earth the peace that is needed.

As we have said before, we are not great; we are here to prepare a way, and in preparing this way for the Messiah, you shall see great miracles performed on your earth.

This is but one of these. There are other children being born on your earth who shall become as this one.

November 27, 1970: *"Is there anything you would like to tell us this evening?"*

Yes, we would say unto thee — one moment, please. Now, that is better, all is in accord.

As we have said before, now is the time of the Cherub. And you say unto us then, and you asked unto us of the book of John. And we say unto you, this is of which we speak.

For there shall be seven angels — and these shall be of the spirit of God, our Father, and yours — and all power shall be placed unto these hands. And one by one the power to give destruction upon your earth shall be given unto these. [See The Revelation of John, chapters 4–22.]

And you say unto us, "What shall happen unto the children of Abraham?" And we should say unto thee, of the children of Abraham, those who were written in the beginning of the Book and those names who shall be added at the end, they shall not perish. But remember, too, man may harm thy bodies — he may inflict wounds upon your body — but man, no man, can destroy the soul or the spirit or the immortal body. Only man himself may do this. [See *The Revelation of John*, chapter 5; 6:9–11; chapter 7; chapter 10; 11:3-4, 19; 13:5-9; 14:1-7, 13-16; 15:2-4; 17:14-15,;19:5-9; 20:4-15; 21:1-27; and 22:1-17.]

"The Revelation of Jesus Christ, which God gave Him to show His servants—things which must shortly take place. And He sent and signified it by His angel to His servant John, who bore witness to the word of God, and to the testimony of Jesus Christ, to all things that he saw. Blessed *is* he who reads and those who hear the words of this prophecy." (*Rev.* 1:1-3)

And remember these words, and the man known as Jesus Christ did speak these words. As he spoke unto Peter he said, "What be it unto you if John should wait until I come again?" And this is of the Book you speak of, for this be the Book of Life, of rebirth and birth again, for in the time of the coming of the Messiah, then our Father shall ask His many children back into His many mansions. [*John* 21:20–24.]

But remember, each soul, each spirit shall come into his Father's light of his own free will. And it will be of his making. And it may be the beggar on the street who shall stand next to our Father, and our Father shall ask of him for advice.

And we say unto thee, cast no stones. For if you must cast a stone, let us stand before thee. [See *John* 8:1-12.]

December 11, 1970: *"Aka, our last question for this evening is from [11–2–70–001]. He asks, 'What activities would you suggest for our family during our Christmas vacation from December 18th to January 4th?'"*

We should say unto thee, we may only open the paths. The path that thy should take should be of thy own free choosing. But remember these things. Take thy family into the desert, teach them of the small things of your earth and the great things of our Father. For remember these words, for there shall be a new heaven and a new earth.

And remember these words,

we are not great, we are only here to prepare a way, for soon shall be the time of the Messiah.

December 18, 1970: *"Thank you, Aka. Have you anything to tell us this evening?"*

35

Yea, now we shall tell thee again of the time of our Lord, your Father, and of a time which was before when our Father was asked to send those who knew of Him.

And now we should tell thee of the ones who should ask, for we should tell thee of the one known as Mohammed; we should tell thee of the one who was known as Buddha; we should tell thee of the one who was known as Jesus Christ; and we should tell you of the many others. We should tell thee of the one who was known as Arcan. Each, in their own way, sought their Father's light. Each, in their own way, reached, as you would know it, the Christ state. Each walked upon your earth.

Now we should tell thee of the many other worlds in which men have reached their Christ state. For if you would think of our Father as the rays of the sun, and the spirits of our Father as the rays of the sun to cast warmness into your souls, cast warmness into your spirit and to shine upon the immortal body of man, and that each man should stand in our Father's light and our Father should enter into this man as the rays of sunshine should enter. But remember also that during the time of darkness our Father may enter into thy minds and thy souls.

Remember also of the goodness that our Father has placed in each man. But, as you would know it, our Father has placed in each man love and hate. Think of this as a saber to cut two ways in each man. Our Father knew that this was necessary for the development of man, for man to be aggressive, for man to be ambitious. All of these things were part of the things our Father placed into man long ago in the creation.

This was giving man his own free will. As man built the towers into the heavens, as he reached forward, step by step, to bring himself from a man-beast into the likeness of our Father, our Father could see of his destructive ways. Yet, our Father forgave His children.

Now you reach a time upon your earth when all of your souls upon your earth think of the blessed time of the birth of Christ, or of Jesus Christ, as you would know him.

Our Father thinks of this time as the births of all Christ in man.

This was the thing that Jesus knew as he lay upon the cross, and died and gave his mortal body into man. But also, this was the thing our Father knew when He took up even the mortal body of the one known as Christ.

Remember, as He gave life into Adam and Adam developed, think thee in this way, that Buddha, that Mohammed, that Jesus Christ were of one. As Jesus went into the wilderness for forty days and nights and tasted temptation, he faced what he had been before. And as the Lamb's blood flowed upon your earth and changed there unto the Holy Spirit, it touched those who would open their heart.

Then take this message into thee for all man to see, to wear it as a shield, not to keep others out of thy heart, but as an entranceway for all mankind.

Only in this way can the seed bear yeast and spread upon your earth, and give love, and do away with this thing known as hatred, and do away with these petty things upon your earth, for only in understanding others may you give this love.

For those who would worship the birth of Christ, remember of his words, "For I have come, not to change what has been upon your earth, but to show you what has been before."

And think thee of these words —

we are not great, we are here only to do the work of our Father and prepare the way for the Messiah of your earth, and then there shall be a new heaven and a new earth.

But remember these words. Your earth shall not die, it shall change, and the people upon your earth shall change with it or perish from your earth.

Can thy understand of which we say?

"I think we do, Aka."

December 28, 1970: Though you walked with us before, you chose rebirth to be on this earth upon this plane that thy love of labor should shine upon the earth in the preparation of the preparing of the way of the coming of the Messiah.

The 1971 messages on Preparing for the Coming

January 8, 1971: Now, we say unto this soul, you ask, in what way may thy serve unto this time again of the coming of a Messiah?...

Take of this gift, not as a burden, but as a burden of love. Give it in a way thy should know of love, for as we have spoke before,

our Father asks thee to give unto Him one tenth of the love He has bestowed upon us, His children.

In many of your worldly churches thy would think of this as material blessings; our Father spoke of it as in love. But accept from another that part of himself which he could have giveth unto thee; accept it and be prepared to forgive those who would trespass upon thee.

February 19, 1971: We have asked that thy form of one by one, and two by two, and three by three, and groups of Thirteen, and Thirteen, and Thirteen beyond. [See *Acts,* chapter 1 and 2:1–41.]

We have told you before that thy time should grow short....
Then we would say unto you, your work has just begun.

Join together as one; build on your earth God's mighty army of minds.

[See *The Revelation*, chapter 19.]

But do not destroy nothing as thy build, only build upon what is there. Do not denounce a man because of his color or his belief. Bring him here to us that we may speak unto him.

As we have told thee before, and thy have not listened and heeded unto our Father's words, if thy brother should offend thee, go to thy brother. But be prepared to forgive yourself, that he may forgive you. Do not hide your feelings, for remember, "the first shall be last and the last shall be first."

Cast God's spirit into the brook. Let it flow to your rivers, and from there to your oceans, and into the many lands.

Let it flow to the leaders of your nations.

Your work, we have told you before, is to prepare the time of the coming of the Messiah. We should say one more word; add this to your name. Place the word of Association before your name. This should place thee all in accord, and as we have said, all in accord with God and in accord with one another.

Work together. Listen to each other.

February 20, 1971: Now all is in accord.

Now we would say unto thee — of this one we called thy instrument, for as three have passed before thee, and as we have said before, "the last shall be first, and the first shall be last;" you have asked this question, "What shall happen to our earth?"

Then we say unto thee, that now thy *have* the last before the first.

Upon the death, as you would know it, of our instrument, until the coming of the Messiah, we shall leave unto thee the spirit. And the spirit shall dwell within the disciples of this work. And this Our Lord, Our Father, has so commanded....

If this work does not succeed upon your earth, then upon our instrument's death you shall have the darkness that arose upon his death and the death of the one known as Jesus Christ.

When Aka's instrument, Ray, died, some of his ashes were placed in his favorite boots and set at the healing springs. He passed on October 5, 2000, during the high, holy Days of Repentance or the Days of Awe. This is just before Yom Kippur, the Day of Atonement, which some call Judgment Day. At this time, people pray that their names will be written in the BOOK of Life.

For you have thought in thy mind of the one known as soul Cayce [Edgar Cayce]; therefore, he was our instrument. This one [Ray Elkins] is our instrument.

And as there were three, and as there were three hours of darkness then, if this work through his disciples does not succeed, we shall give your earth three hundred years of darkness. We shall give your earth a time of barbarian, of killing — of all things.

For as we have said before, now is the time of the Cherub.

One crucified on a cross next to Jesus, a thief, rebuked the other criminal for taunting Jesus, and asked Jesus to remember him when he comes to his throne. Jesus answered, "I tell you this: today you shall be with me in Paradise." [See Luke 23:35–47.]

Now we give unto you this time — in the year of 1998. Then we shall spare thee by two years. If all is not in completion for the arrival of the Messiah upon your earth, and peace, the wrath of the Lord into His seven angels shall spill forth.

[Please note: Jesus said, "But of that day and hour no one knows, not even the angels of heaven, but My Father only." (Matthew 24:36.)

Have we been given the grace of more time from our Father in His love? This work of the preparation for the coming of the Messiah continues today, of which Aka speaks above. They have been sent to prepare the way for the Messiah's coming, first within our hearts. Ray said, for his last 27 years, even before he died in 2000 during the high, holy Days of Repentance or of Awe, that it hasn't been decided yet which way the world will go.]

There shall be many messages.

For those, we should say unto now, who are prepared to give into their lives unto the Lord, do so.

For those who should not who we have brought forth into commandment, then we should wipe from thy mind all that has transpired, that you may go forth as sheep upon your earth.

But remember, you must live again, these sheep. What you do unto this day forth, records shall be kept. If thy throw stones, stones shall be cast back. All that we have given unto you, we should take back. For as the Lamb has said before, 'Go unto this house and give blessing. If you are rejected, take back your blessing.'

April 23, 1971: And we shall tell thee of the time.

And in this time, your heaven and earth stood still, for God stretched our His mighty hand and touched your earth. And as He touched your earth, a Messiah was born unto the one known as Mary.

And you asked unto us, "Has this happened before?" Then we say unto thee, our Father has touched your earth many times in many places, for is it not written that the beggar on the street should be the next one to stand next to God, and God should ask his advice of many things.

Then you say unto us, "If God, our Father, is so powerful, why, then, should He ask the advice of a beggar?" And we say unto you, would it not be that a wise man to take counsel, even on your earth? For our Lord should weigh all things.

And you say unto us, "Then why should our Lord let wars rage on your earth? Why should men be allowed to kill each other?"

And we should say unto thee, our Lord gave unto thee free choice, free choice unto all. Even as the spirit form knows of God, you were given free choice. Even unto the soul, you were given free choice. And even into the body form of the man beast, you were given free choice. For as you climb the ladder back to our Father, even there you should have free choice.

For did our Father not say unto thee, "Come unto me as a child, for this is what I give unto you." [See *Mark* 9:30–37.]

And what was meant is as a child is born upon your earth, he is born within sin, without karma.

Then you say unto us, "How could this be so?"

And we say unto thee, through the free choice our Father has given you. In that proportion of your brain that you think of nothingness, there lies the memory of all life forms. There shall be planted and planted again, all your planes.

Then you would say unto us, "Without memory, how then can we correct our karma, or sin?"

Remember these words, our Father gives unto thee the earth. Our Father gives unto thee life. Man maketh the world, and so, on earth it shall be in heaven. Can thy understand of which we speak? Nay, not fully, for we see doubt.

Then we say unto thee, go ye upon your earth and see new life at birth, even into the smallest creature upon your earth, not one shall fall or rise again without the permission of God.

Yet, has He not said unto you, "in our kind and in our likeness," for what father would want his child to be so complete that he could be a precise image of himself? Nay. And this is the reason God placed unto thee the Godhead of man. This is what was meant, "in our kind and in our likeness." [See *Genesis* 1:26–27.]

And within time, man upon your earth shall come to know the true meaning of these words and the true love of his Father.

But God shall weep for His children. But they should come back into His many mansions. But as with the smallest thing of your earth, God gives love and life unto all, for He is the God of the living, not the dead....

[Aka spoke to a woman]: We see that thy tasks shall grow even more as a burden, but remember, it is a burden of love,

> *for if a place should be made ready upon your earth for the coming of the Messiah, then many hands shall be needed and many minds.*

For have we not said before, all that is covered shall be lighted again, and not one stone upon your earth shall not be turned, for our Lord's hand is again upon thy earth.

Can thy understand of which we speak?

"*I think so,*" [she answers.]

May 2, 1971: And now, we should tell thee again of the time of the Anti-Christ. For soon upon your earth all things shall change, for men should burn and steal and kill, and darkness shall come upon your earth.

> *But the children of God shall fear not, for the angels shall hover above your earth and gather, as once before, the lambs of earth.*

And those who resist the mark of the Beast shall live again in God's kingdom. And for those who shall wear the mark of the God, and who were in the Book of the beginning and who are in the Book of this time, for their descendants, our Father has promised a thousand years of peace upon your earth. But remember, this time shall come, not as you count, but as our Father should count.

And once again, the Messiah shall walk your earth and give blessings.

[See *The Revelation*, chapters 12–22.]

But it shall be different, for now we shall give thee this message. For as before, the Messiah walked in five placed, he shall not this time upon this coming. And for those who should wear the mark of Christ, the Lamb, their descendants and their descendants forevermore shall dwell in the house of the Lord. And temptation shall be taken from their path, for at this time that that dwells in man, which is Lucifer, shall be no more.

And all the Jewish people of the earth shall bow before Christ.

[See *Zechariah* 12:9–14.]

And you ask, "How can this be possible?" And we say unto you in this manner. For our God, our Lord, can change the descendants of man as you can turn a stone, for this word, as we have said before, for as God's spirit flows as a brook, as man's spirit flows as a river, as the souls of man should flow as an ocean to the many lands, to the many nations, to the many tongues, and all shall become as one.

But remember these words. Our Father and yours, our God, has many mansions. All man was given free choice. God asks that you should love of Him one-tenth of the love that He should give unto you, and He asks that thee love of thy fellow man.

And we should say unto thee, prepare thee for the famine. Store of the food for each man, woman and child upon thy earth; store food for one year of your calendar. Store seeds that thy may replant and replenish the earth. Store the seed of knowledge that thy may take this [on] to thy descendants of all forms. Store pure drinking water, and this should be done to sustain you for six months. Store farm implements; tools of all nature and kind.

Can thy understand of which we speak?

"Yes, Aka."

May 7, 1971:

Take into thy heart and thy soul the blessings of others. Form thy life in giving unto others.

Remember, for was it not written before that our Father and yours loved His many children. But we would say that our Father should choose the beggar upon the street to stand and ask advice, for there are many who have reached the Christ state, and there shall be many more.

But remember, also, that we are here to prepare a way for the coming of the Messiah.

If thy should make unto thyself the sign of the ankh, in thy meditation we should come unto thee and give thee blessings, and therefore, give thee teachings.

Can thy understand of which we speak?

Nay, not fully. Then we would say unto these words. Tonight as thy should sleep in thy slumber, we should send one who should speak unto thee.

May 14, 1971: Then we would say these things into thee. Our coming was not meant to cause fear or confusion into thee; our coming was for the preparation for the coming of the Messiah.

Therefore, we would say these words into thee, blessed are those who may wait. Blessed are those with patience. Blessed are the flowers [followers] of our Father. But remember, as we have said before, we shall allow no one to interfere with this work, for remember, we may do nothing without our Father's permission. Can thy understand of which we speak?

"Yes, Aka."

Then we would say unto thee,

cast not a stone, but only a blessing upon your earth.

As we have told thee before, in the preparation of our coming, much work was needed, much work was needed in the choosing of our instrument, in the readiness of the same. There is much work yet to be done. When we tell thee of the time of thy needs, we do not expect thee to run like sheep, but stand firm as the Lamb in the Lamb's light. Give of the healing where it is needed, both mentally and physically. Give blessings where they are accepted. But where they are not accepted, then take back thy blessings and knock upon another door....

We see in thy mind many questions. These questions we should answer into thee, and all shall become just and fair. But remember of our promise unto thy descendants.

The star shall be kept, but keep thy vows into our Father, for in your time thy shall see the coming of the Messiah.

56

You shall see your world bow before him. And our Father shall give all thy descendants blessings.

May 21, 1971: Remember these words; thy needs, as we have promised of the material nature, shall be taken care of. But do not grow greedy; do not ask for too much, for as raindrops, these things that thy should need shall be furnished unto thee.

For remember, we are not great, we are here to prepare a way for the coming of the Messiah.

Can thy understand of which we speak?

May 28, 1971: And now, as before, we should tell thee of this time, and they who should walk through the valley of our Lord, and so sayeth the Lord, that "I SHOULD SEND SEVEN ANGELS INTO THE SEVEN CHURCHES OF YOUR EARTH to dwell there and give guidance," and "blessed is those who should walk by the side of the Lord."

(See *The Revelation*, chapters 8–11.)

But now, the Lamb sayeth into thee, "What for art thou who has deserted me? What for art thou who should in his own words denyeth the Lord and the spirit unto which we have left upon your earth?"

For, as we have said before, the last shall be first, and the first shall be last. So, as our Father has commanded, you have had the last, and now thy should have unto thee the first.

For those who should say unto the Lord, as into the time of Abraham, "Oh, Lord, why have Thy asked to [lose, use] me upon this earth? Why have Thy asked to desert me upon this earth?"

And the Lord sayeth unto thee, "LOOK FORTH INTO YOUR FUTURE, FOR I, AS YOUR LORD, HAVE GIVEN UNTO THEE WISDOM, HAVE GIVEN UNTO THEE FREE CHOICE."

And thy say unto the Lord, "Why have Thy forsaken our churches? Why doest Thee among us turn away?"

And the Lord sayeth unto thee, as in the time of Isaiah, "ALL THINGS UPON THY EARTH MUST CHANGE."

Man must change, and the earth must change, for as we should plant into your earth the seed to grow, and the seed should grow of good fruit, yet bear bad fruit, pick from this tree the bad fruit and cast it into the pit. Pick from this good fruit and lay it away for seed to grow again upon your earth. And as each year should pass, and the new fruit should bear fruit again, your earth should be fruitful in the eyes of the Lord. But nay, thy have not done unto us the same. Thy have planted again unto thy earth of the bad fruit.

And now, we say unto you of this time, your half-times have ended, and now shall be the full time of the Lord, for the Lord should send unto your earth those who should pick of the fruit. And of the bad fruit, He should cast into the pit of nothingness. And of the good fruit, He should plant again in the orchard of your new Messiah.

And we say unto these of the churches of your earth, prepare thee the way for the Messiah. Prepare thee a way that our Lord should fill His many mansions with His children again.

"YEA, YEA," sayeth the Lord unto thee, "COME INTO MY HOUSE AND DWELL AND DRINK, AND I SHOULD COME INTO THINE AND DWELL AND DRINK, AND GIVE BLESSINGS INTO THY CHILDREN'S CHILDREN."

For upon your earth, the rivers shall flow again in this time.

For those who would walk away from the Lord, we should say unto thee, the time of the great Sword is here — now. Where water flowed, no water shall flow again of this time. Prepare thy earth for the time of the drought. Plant of the seed that should grow upon your earth. Put away thy harvest, thy harvest of knowledge, thy harvest of fruits.

For upon your earth our Lord has promised unto thee a new earth and a new heaven —

and as our Lord is always truthful, and as our Lord should say, as in the time of Abraham and in the time of the king of Peace, as thy would know, in the time of Salem, for as Abraham had no one to give true tribute to, he did give unto this, this king of Salem, one-tenth and one-tenth into all the souls.

Can thy understand of which we speak?

Nay, not fully, but thy shall, for in thy hearts new fields shall be harvested and new tongues shall be spoken....

[Spoken to one]: And these words our Father should say unto thee, "PREPARE YOUR EARTH FOR THE COMING OF THE MESSIAH, AND YOUR MISSION SHALL BE COMPLETE."

Prepare thy earth in such a manner that they should greet him as their savior, and not as thy slave.

If thee should do of our bidding, then our Father should give of thee and thy descendants the help that is needed. And upon these words we should say of this vow —

forever upon your earth shall be peace….

"Aka, [   ] asks…'I want to understand what God's plan for me is….'

As thy walk forth in thy daily life, shine forth the light of our Father. Let it come from thy heart, and thy eyes, and thy mouth when thy speak, and therefore, the time of the Cherub shall not be wasted,

for let it go forth into the time of the Messiah.

For as we have said before, place before thee the sign of the ankh. Wear it in proud reverence of thy work, and think unto it as the sun's rays come upon thy earth, and from thy body, let it flow forever inward, but though it should flow inward, let it flow outward. Do not imprison this source. Can thy understand of which we speak?

"Yes, Aka."

June 11, 1971: As we have said before, now is the time of the Cherub.

> *And for the one who should ask our Father — and that that has been said before shall be said again — for we are not great; we are here to prepare a way for the coming of your Messiah.*

Where no light did shine before, light shall shine again. Upon your earth shall become new again, and therefore, there shall be a new heaven and a new earth. For as the rivers flow, so shall the mighty force of our Lord flow upon your earth.

As we have said before, now is the time of the Cherub, for now the seven angels dwell above your earth. [See *The Revelation,* chapters 4–22.]

And think not that we of the Thirteen should sit in judgment, for we are not here for that purpose. We are here to prepare the minds of men for the time that the Messiah should come upon your earth, and to fulfill the words that were spoken by our Lord when He did promise unto thee a thousand years of peace. But remember, this time shall come not as you count, but as our Father, your God, your Father, did count.

And as He made thee this coveth, all of the heaven opened upon your earth, for did He not promise unto thee, "For thee should be in our likeness, of our kind?"

[See *The Revelation*, chapters 19–22; *Acts*, chapters 1–2; and *Genesis* 1:26–28.]

You think not that the words spoken unto thee are new? Nay.

"Nay," sayeth the Lord.

These words are not new, for has not a new Book been written? And did He not promise that all those in the Book of the beginning, and were in the Book of the ending, therefore, should live forever, and therefore, eat from His table and drink of His wine? [See *The Revelation,* chapters 19–22.]

Then look out among you. Cast no stones, for remember, you can destroy nothing upon your earth, for all things come from the same source. You may only change its form, as the Lord changed the form of each animal upon your earth, and the fowl that flies upon the earth, and all things within the earth.

June 18, 1971: But beware. Beware of the other side, for as Atlantis did rise and fall, so did the souls of man.

For remember, worlds have their karma, and each country and country within the country should have of these karmas. Therefore, it should be placed into thy hands, that of which to overcome of the same,

for thy shall be as once before in the time of the coming of the Messiah.

And we should say unto thee, carry this blessing forward, for in thy life span we should speak unto thee many times. And we should extend thy days. But be blessed, for there is none that can be greater than the teacher, and the teacher can be no greater than the pupil.

June 25, 1971, Aka said to one: Through prayer and meditation, bring thyself in accord with this one thy would know of Jesus Christ, for thy will see the time again of his entry, for were there not those who choose to remain upon the earth, and therefore, be here again in the coming of the Messiah? For your earth, to save this earth, did he not die once?

Were you not there; do you not remember? Does not this dwell in thy heart and soul? Look deeply into thyself. If still thy cannot remember, then we should come into thee in thy dreams and help thee and send thee further teachers.

Can thy understand of which we speak?

"Not completely." [He answers.]

Then go unto thy slumbers, and we shall enter. Fear us not, for we mean thee no harm.

June 30, 1971: Yes, we see thy need. Then we say unto thee of thy question. First, we should say unto thee, remember unto these words our Father has spoken,

for the prophecies of the Lord shall flow upon your earth as your rivers, and from your rivers into the mighty oceans and to the many lands.

Thy have asked this question, and so permission has been given to answer of the same.

Of your first question, we say unto thee, we are not mighty. We are but the messengers of your Father, your God.

Thy ask, are we but angels? And we say unto thee, this word of yours, angels, is a word that was manifested by those of your own. We are but instruments of our Father. Our Father sent us for those who have reached the Christ state and for those who would prepare the way for the coming of the Messiah. We were the first upon your earth, and as the first, and the last shall be first.

There are some among us who have walked upon many of your worlds. But all of us have walked upon the three sisters.

We were chosen for this work not because we are greater than others. Unlike your instrument, we have lived many lives. But even before your world, think thee of the time when your planet, Mars, came very close to your earth, and of the time when what you know as meteorites and asteroids passed inward into thy earth, for we were there.

And think thee of the time when our Lord created your earth and your universes, for we have said unto thee before that thy earth comes from one source.

We have told thee of the time of the cosmos and of the beginning. Therefore, think thee about your sun, for there is not an ending, but of a beginning. And think thee of the twelve sisters of your earth, and of the Thirteen, for there lies the timetable yet to unfold unto mankind, for it has unfolded before. For your Earth returns back to the beginning and then, therefore, is created a new earth.

But your mankind, as you would know it, has lived on many planets, in many universes.

For our Father has made His vow unto man that man shall not perish.

He may walk away from his knowledge, for he is granted free choice. Then think thee of these words, for is it not written that from the firmament did grow all things, and from the heaven and the earth did not God breathe life into the same.

July 1, 1971: We have come to [R   ]. All she must do is think of us each evening, and we will be there. It does not have to be evening; at any time, day or night, we are there.

For you must realize, for from where we come there is no day or night.

Can you understand this?

"Yes."

Now we would tell you of a time which was before, when men with hate and greed destroyed the things they loved most, of the time of Atlantis. And by telling you of this time, you will know what can happen again. For all the knowledge that came to them was buried beneath the earth, there to remain.

As we have said before, this knowledge is soon, all parts of it, shall rise again. What was dark shall be lighted. What was buried shall be uncovered. For, as we have said before, now is the time of the Cherub.

For we are here to prepare a way, for we seek a place that the Messiah may enter.

The time that he shall be known to you grows close; therefore, our time grows smaller.

If thy would look at the last words that Christ, Jesus, said before he left his physical body, then to return to it, you will understand of what we speak of....

[See Jesus' farewell discourses, *John* 13–17.]

To each of you, as thy pray for help and guidance, help is sent, help to look after one soul or a group of souls. Fear this not; this is good.

Can thy understand this?

"Yes, thank you."

Jesus' last Passover supper

July 17, 1971: And now, as we have said before, in the time of Atlantis, the Lord came into Noah, and did say unto [he], "Build thee an ark, and take those of those of thy own, who have held in their memory God, their creator, and go thee unto a new land."

And they made preparations for the ship they were to travel in.

He did say unto them, "Go forward, and not backward," as He did say unto the people of your time, of your plane.

Remember of these words, for as He spoke unto the people of Israel words that they could understand, and now He speaks unto *you* words that you can understand.

Then we say unto thee, go forward; go forward into this new time.

But do not bury thy knowledge. Do not bury it, so that in a different world people will seek backward into time to try to find this knowledge to bring it into light. For knowledge is not a sin, for God placed all things on thy earth to be used by man.

Did He not make man the master of this earth of yours?

Did He not give man the universes upon universes?

For as He created man of His kind, of His likeness, and He did create he and she, one never to be greater than the other — for remember, be a pupil first and then a teacher, and thy shall grow into that likeness of our Lord, and of that kind, of our Lord.

But thy cannot do this by burying thy heads in the sand. [See *Genesis* 1:26–31.]

If thy grow a tree, and it grows good in the firment of your soil, and as thy harvest the tree thy take of its best fruit, and therefore, seed, year by year, these thy should plant again shall grow into a better fruit. And man should be of the same, for all this is in God's plan for man.

And did He not promise unto thee a new heaven and a new earth? All these things should come.

[See The Revelation *21:1–8.]*

But as we have said before, if thy right eye should offend thee, cast it aside. [See *Mark* 9:43–50.]

But then, do not go backward to pick it up and use it again. Leave it there. Walk away from this, and go forward. This should be done with thy knowledge also.

*In **Angels Give a Glimpse through All Time: Past-life readings told from 1970–1989 (Book with Wings**, volume 2) Aka gives many more messages about the "coming of the Messiah" before, in the past, and looking forward to this time.*

Benefit by what has happened in the past. This is why we have given unto thee the knowledge, thy would call, in thy life readings. This is why we have given unto thee the knowledge of your past civilizations. And of your question upon Atlantis, we should say unto thee, within time Atlantis shall rise again beneath the sea and the ice, for Atlantis was in your northern hemisphere. And as the axis of the earth turned, these people fled unto a land much liking to their own.

And as God gave man the earth to ferment and plant his seed upon, and therefore, to replenish the earth, so He did in this time. For all things that have been before shall be again.

For remember, we are not great. We are here for one purpose, that purpose is to prepare a way that God's children may return back to their many mansions. And for this to be done, we must prepare a way for the coming of the Messiah.

There are many things thy do not understand. Be not afraid to ask, and this knowledge shall be given unto thee.

July 23, 1971: Then we should say unto you these words. There shall be chaos. And as thy enter into the time of the Fourth Angel, then we should say unto you these words. We have given unto you this work to carry from the brook to the rivers, and out into the oceans of time, that it may be carried to the many lands. [See *The Revelation* 6:7–17 and chapter 7.]...

But there are others in the isles of California who should serve unto the Lord's work.

And as in the time of Abraham, show us but one soul, and we should spare of the many.

The San Andreas fault in California shows where two continental plates collide as the Pacific plate pushes northward and the North American plate moves southward. Some predict that the "Big One" will come with eruptions, earthquakes and possibly islands forming to the west that may rise and sink back into the ocean.

But we say unto thee, there is many there who should work of the psychic, and they have not heeded our words. Then we say unto thee, that the stone that was thrown into the brook should pass into the rivers and to your oceans, and as we have said before, not one stone upon your earth shall be left unturned. Then bring these forth unto us. Can you understand of which we speak?

"No."

Then we would say unto thee, bring unto us one soul, that the work of our Father may be implanted, that those souls who dwell in these isles may be given these words, and therefore, be prepared for the coming of the Messiah, but therefore, to be prepared for that day unto which the Seventh Angel shall drop his mighty sword upon your earth. If this is done, then our Lord shall spare many, for they must wash their clothes in the Lamb's blood, for they must make their body and souls cleansed and purified in the light of the Lord. Can you understand of which we speak? [See *The Revelation,* chapters 8–11, 14–22.]

"Yes."...

But remember of these words. Thine are the temple of God, for as our Lord has said before, thy were created "in our likeness, of our kind." And as the [firmament] of the earth and the [firmament] of the sky came together, then life was breathed into thy body. But remember of this, as the Creator, all substances upon thy earth, above it and below it, were all created from the same source. [See *Genesis* 1:26–31.]

Think thy of a time when men of thine species, as thy would know it, could have saddled then their energy of the earth itself. This shall be done again. And thy of thy people shall then have a choice, as the people of Atlantis did have.

Shall you use this creative force, then, for the welfare of mankind or shall you again cast Atlantis below the sea?

But our Lord has promised unto thee a thousand years of peace. This time shall come upon thy earth, and the Messiah shall come again.

This Messiah shall not come until man is ready to receive him in the manner our Lord should prepare for him.

Then go unto thy earth and give of these words and blessings, for thy shall be empowered with the casting away of demons, as thy would know it, for there are many of these upon thy earth that must be chained and cast into the endless pit. [See *The Revelation*, chapter 20.]

But we say unto thee, do not take of our words, as has been done before, and turn them into thy own need; for if thy should do of this, then we should cut, as the Lord has done before, of thy right hand.

[Editor's note: The earliest record found of scripture of the ancient Hebrew is a stone on which is inscribed the Lord's cutting of the right hand.]

Thy have other questions, ask.

"Yes, Aka. You spoke of contacting souls in California to get them to work for the coming of the Messiah, if I understood you correctly. Do you have in mind a certain person or certain manner in which you wish us to do this, or do you encourage a group effort in this? How shall we go about this?"

We shall say unto thee, if thy could do this of thyselves, thy should be that much closer to the communications of thy Father, thy Lord. And as our Father has given thee free choice, so He shall. Then do this of thy own will, of thy own free choice. If from time to time, thy should have difficulty, remember, our Lord stands behind thee in guidance and deliverance of the same.

"Yes, Aka. The question has been asked by one of our group, 'What is the meaning of the blood of the Lamb, being washed in the blood of the Lamb?'"

For, as before, the Lamb should be of the Messiah.

And as he was pure into the light of the Lord, and as the blood that flowed from his body upon his crucifixion and touched your earth, and therefore, made it pure, therefore, as thy would wash thy clothes in the blood of the Lamb, if thy could wash thyselves in the blood of the Lamb,

he left unto your earth of the Holy Spirit.

He told unto you, 'I have not come to change the Law, but to show you of its fulfillment.' Therefore, in his passing was he not resurrected into life again?

And these same things, as thy climb the ladder to be born and born again, and as thy of thy own free choice, as he did, choose to enter over again, and enter in the pure light of his Father, so should you —

if thy build upon this earth the temple of man, the temple of God within man.

We do not ask of thee to build to our Lord of a great building.

We asked that thy build His temple within man, for as the body should waste away, then therefore, this temple can be built again within three days.

August 15, 1971: *"Is there anything you would like to tell us this evening?"*

We see thy need. Therefore, we should say upon these words. Thy have spoke many times of thy churches, thy places of worship unto the Lord, and we have said unto thee these words, for the temple of God is in man. For the churches of thy worship do not make the man, the man brings the temple of God into thy churches, and therefore, places his place of worship into the Lord.

Thy have many questions, ask.

"Yes, Aka, the question has come up that on the different nights of your coming there are different voices. Are we right in this belief?"

We should say unto thee these words. For as there is a council of Thirteen, and as we have told unto thee these words —

there are many souls, many spirits, as we were sent for the one who asked —

for the council of Thirteen, this is made up of many spirits, as thy would know them.

But remember also, we are not great. For our coming, permission must be given from our Lord, our Father. But we should say of these words of our coming, we are here to prepare a way for the coming of the Messiah.

[See *John* 14:1–5, 14:15–28, 16:6–15, chapter 17, and *Acts* 1:6–26, 2:1–28.]

And we should say these words unto thee. Thy shall live through the dark ages again, for upon our coming also came the time of the Cherub.

And the Fourth Angel is upon thy earth. For famine, for the infection thy have placed upon the earth of our God, not one stone upon thy earth shall be left unturned.

But your earth shall not end. Your earth shall go on, for our Father has promised into thee a new heaven and a new earth.

And for the children of our Father, there shall be a thousand years of peace upon your earth.

But remember also, this is as our Father should count.

For the wise to hear and the wise to learn.

For this also is the time of the coming of the anti-Christ, and his name should be of six times sixty-six, as it is written upon the records of time. [See *The Revelation,* chapters 4 through 8, 12, 13, 14:, 15:1–4, 19 through 22.]

In thy study of astrology thy should think upon the 12 months of the year; but think thee upon the 24 months of the year, for this was as it is in the beginning, and so it should be in the ending.

August 29, 1971: And we should say these words into thee. For we are not great.

We are but the messengers of God, our Father. We are here for but one purpose, to prepare for the coming of the Messiah....

For as it has been said before, what has covered shall be uncovered; where no light shone light shall shine again.

But as we have said before, at times, to translate, as you would say, from your plane to ours is very difficult.

And as you have asked before of the council of Thirteen, and as we have said before, do not misinterpret our words.

For once before, as in the time of Adam, man was created in five places, and this [were] the sons of God. And yet, many entries went into the man-beast and these were the sons of man. And as the men of God looked unto the daughters of man and saw them fair, and therefore, did enter into the same, thy were cast out of thy Garden of Eden, and therefore, thy created death. [See *Genesis,* chapters 2–7.]

For remember, our Father is the God of the living, not of the dead.

And so, we come once again, but not in five places, but in one — therefore, as the spirits of God flows as pebbles, as the spirit of man should flow as the pebbles of a river, as the souls of man should flow as the pebbles of an ocean, unto the many lands unto the many tongues.

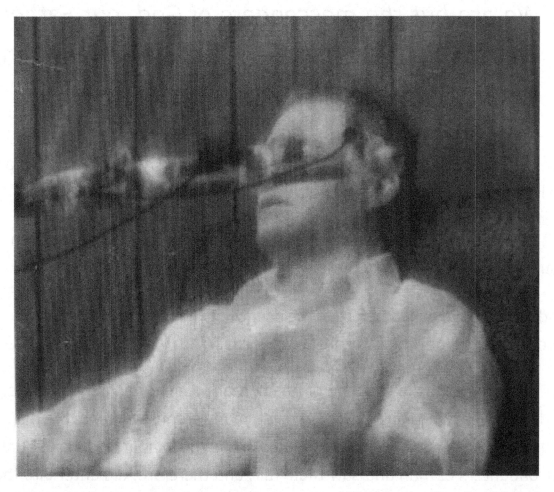

Can you see the spiritual messengers of God, Aka, as rays of light flowing like a brook into the unconscious body of Ray — after he had left his body to walk up a ladder to stand with God, so they could enter and speak to us? The infinite rays of light of God's spiritual messengers shine from "many galaxies, many universes and worlds beyond worlds" to enter his body and are with and in him as they speak. Microphones of a stand partly obscure the face in this photo that was taken as Aka spoke one evening in 1973. [See John 14:1–28, 15:26–27, 16:5–15, 17:20–26.]

And as we have said before, this is not the time of Lot, for we come upon your plane upon your time. [See *Genesis*, chapter 19.]

But as we have said before, the half-times are over. Now is the time of our Lord.

And as we have said before, do not misinterpret our words. Thy cannot drive half of a calf to market, nor can you take half of a word and receive a meaning. If there are stones to cast, let us stand before thee, and cast thy first stone at us.

Thy ask in thy mind of this 29th day of your August, and as we told thee before to think of the 24 months, and not of your 12 — we have told thee of the beginning of the Fourth Angel upon your earth. And so it shall be. And we have told thee of your free choice, which neither our Father or us may interfere with.

We have given unto thee these messages, that you, with your free choice, might alter the events or catastrophe that should destroy thy earth within itself.

If thy have no faith, and as our Lord did say unto thee, "if thy eye should offend thee, cast it aside."

But we should say again unto these words, for that that was placed into the earth should come from the earth, and that that was placed into the sea should come from the sea. And that that belongs to the earth shall stay in the earth, and that that belongs to God shall stay with God. And that that belongs to Lucifer shall stay with Lucifer. But should a man kill another with a sword, so should he be killed with a sword, for that in itself is karma. But do not blame your Father for your own shortcomings. [See *The Revelation* 6:7–8, chapters 7–8, and *Mark* 9:43–48.]

September 16, 1971: *"All right. At this time, Aka, we have no other written question. Is there any information you would like to give us?"*

Yes, we see this.

Then we should answer the question of before. [9–16–71–001]

For her God, for our Father, is the creator of the universes and galaxies and planets. For remember, her Father loves His many children. But as we have said before that as each individual should have free choice and that each person upon thy earth should worship their God in their own way, for our Father did not set down rules of worship unto Himself,

> *for He asks only that thy should have no other god before Him, and that thy should love thy God unto one-tenth that of which He loves His children, and that thy* should love of thy fellow man unto the same as thy love thy God.

And thy say in thy mind, "Where is this God?" Then we should say unto thee these words. Thy God is everywhere. And in yourselves our God does dwell, for in that proportion of yourself thy should call thy conscience, and in this word thy use so often, yet know not the meaning of, in that word of love.

For if thy should doubt of our Father, look at thyself....

And we should tell thee of these words. For our Father and His son did promise unto man that before the Seventh Angel should strike thy earth He should send two prophets upon thy earth — and therefore, to prepare a way for the coming of the Messiah.

And as the prophets of before, beware, for this One thy should not stone again. [See *The Revelation* 11:1-13.]

But we should say unto thee these words. If a prophet should come unto thee and speak of our Father in an untruth manner, and he comes not of the Spirit, then beware. [See *Matthew* 24:3-6, 23-27.]

For our Father has seen fit to place upon [this] earth the new Book. And this Book should have wings. And for those who have ears to listen, then hark of our Father should say unto thee. For if thy should dwell upon the earth, wear not the mark of the beast. [see *The Revelation* 20:4-15.]

But for those who have come to say our Father is not merciful — for these are not the children of God. For remember, not one stone upon thy earth shall be left unturned. [See *Matthew* 24:1–3.]

As written in the introduction to this writing, the spiritual messengers of God said, September 24, 1971: And as we have said before, we are not great. We are here for but one purpose, to prepare the way for the coming of the Messiah — and that he may walk upon holy ground.

Then we should say unto thee these words. Blessed are they who should worship unto our Father. Blessed are they who should give unto the poor. And blessed are they who should give glory unto our Father this day.

For hark, we should say unto thee these words. For [sHe] should give unto thee a new Book upon this day….

But we should say unto thee these words. As a woman should give birth unto a child, so should our Lord give birth unto your minds. And as the pain is great before the birth, but therefore, upon the birth and the knowledge of new birth upon thy earth, this should give thee great joy, and therefore, thy should forget of the pain that came before the birth. [See *John* 16:18–24.]

Therefore, our Father should place great joy upon thy minds.

It matters [not, of naught] to our Father that thy should climb His ladder slowly. But what does matter to our Father is your struggles to climb it at all. And therefore, should you give glory unto our Father, our Father, therefore, gives glory unto His children.

And we should say unto thee these words. Was not the one known as Jesus Christ, did not God prefer that he be born upon your earth, that he come into the world as a man-beast? And therefore, as we have said before, even our Father has learned from experience.

For as before, as the sons of God found the daughters of man fair and did enter, and therefore, bring forth upon thy earth the children of God, and as your Father did bring upon your earth His firstborn child, and therefore, to show unto His children the truth of our Father's Law, and to fulfill the prophecies of the prophet[s] — and therefore, once again these prophecies shall be fulfilled upon thy earth.

And we should say unto thee these words. We have much knowledge; we have many messages that we should give unto thee from our Father. Be patient, for as good wine should take time to make, so should the knowledge of God in the telling take time.

October 15, 1971: And we should say unto these words, for we see thy need, soul John, and we have seen thy travels and been with thee. And we should give unto this one, as once before, the gift of waiting.

For as we have said before, we are not great; we are here but for one reason, to prepare the way for the coming of the Messiah.

[See *John* 21:20–24.]

We cannot interfere with thy free choice. We can only but knock on thy door, and await thy entering. If thy beckon unto us, we may enter. If thy should close the door and make us wait, this we should do, but only for a short while. For our time grows short, and therefore, we need unto thee thy [help]. We have given unto thee the power to heal; use this power. Use it readily. But heal first of the soul, and then of the body....

If thy should walk upon the water with us, have faith, for we have faith in thee. Have faith in God, for He loves His children so. And yet, He weeps.

And He says unto His children, "MUST I WEEP FOREVER? MUST I SHOW MY WRATH WHEN IN MY HEART THERE IS BUT LOVE?"

Remember, now is the time of the Cherub, and we are here but for one purpose, to prepare a way for the coming of the Messiah.

Let this time be a time of gladness. And let God's children have before them the hands of welcome.

For only with the use of your own free will can this happen.

November 9, 1971: We shall say unto thee these words.

We are here but for one purpose – that is in the preparation for the preparing of the coming of the Messiah.

We have selected those who should help, one by one, and two by two, and three by three. We still search for those who should make up of the thirteen. To each of these, we have given triste and trial. For some have fell along the way. For in the time of the one known as Jesus, there were thirteen. And one did fall. This cannot be. Each person who is chosen *must* be ready to give their lives, as you would know them, for God. [See *John*, chapters 16–18 and *Acts*, chapter 1.]...

For those who we have chosen we have given unto those the ability to heal. We have given unto these great powers. But as we have said before, the Lord should giveth and the Lord should taketh away.

We shall ask thee to be patient, to let us bring healing into thyselves, to let us change thy paths, and therefore, bring the love of the Lord into thy heart and soul.

But remember, we can do nothing without our Father's permission, for we are not great. We are but the messengers of our Lord. For we have been before your time, and we shall be again after your time. But remember, too, the half-times are over.

November 12, 1971: Yet, we should give unto thee the knowledge and the guidance that is needed. And fear not, for as we should come into thy home, all thy must do for guidance is to open the door, that we may enter.

Remember, we are not great. We are here but to prepare the way for the coming of the Messiah. We may do nothing that our Father does not allow; we may tell thee nothing that our Father does not allow, for we are the servants and the messengers of our Father. [See *John* 16:13–15.]

November 16, 1971: We shall take care of the other needs of thy body. We shall give healing into the same. But remember, we are not great. We may only do these things that our Father permits us to do, for we are the servants of God, our Father, and we are here for but one purpose, to prepare the way for the coming of the Messiah.

Therefore, we should ask in return, make fallow his bed.

November 26, 1971:

"A_____ R____, who is here tonight, asks, 'What is the basis of my dread of Christmas this year?'"

Yes, we see thy need. And we should answer in this manner. Thy dread of Christmas is the dread of the gifts thy should receive. But fear not, for remember, accept a gift as it is given with love. Do not enter into that proportion that is given from those with false faces. Send them love unto the same. Ask in thy prayers that we may enter, and we should enter, therefore, and give guidance and healing into the same.

But as your Christmas is a time to celebrate the birth of the one known as Jesus, and of a gift from God unto you, and as man chose to give gifts unto this one known as Jesus, he has chosen to give gifts to one another.

Quite often we lose sight of the true art of giving. For remember, you are the children of God. Therefore, the Lord should look into thy needs, and therefore, give a gift into *thee* in a manner that will be most marvelous for thy eyes to see.

But fear not, for we see no sin. Remember these words, what is sin to man is not sin to God. You have made many rules, therefore, to worship our Lord, and your Father.

But remember, as you celebrate the coming of the Messiah, we are here but for one purpose – that is in the preparation for the coming of the Messiah upon your earth. But remember, not only your earth shall celebrate this, for in all the galaxies that thy can think of, they shall celebrate this also.

For as the Lord should change a stone, so should this happen on your earth —

for in the preparation we are here to open the doors of your souls. We are here to build the temple of God in man.

November 30, 1971: And as we have said before that peace shall come unto your earth, and therefore, you shall be given your thousand years of peace upon the earth; but as we have said before, this shall not be as you count, but as God counts, therefore, for as a day shall be as a thousand years,

hark, then and hear these words.

For the Red Horse stands ready to do destruction into your country. Unless the proper precautions are taken, an attempt will be made in February, of your month, of your time, of your calendar, upon the life of the President of your country [U.S.A.].

Therefore, we say unto thee these words, hark. And war shall come upon your land, but fear not, for it shall be lean in time. And as we have said before, peace shall come.

But beware of the Brown Horse, for in this land thy know as South America, and in this land thy know as the Panamas and the Mexico, there shall be a new threat unto your earth.

For beware, for as you land was given unto God and given unto man as a new beginning, and as you brought your past with you forward into time, then we shall tell thee in these words, and at the present time they may seem as riddles unto thee.

For as we have spoke before of the coming of the Messiah, so should he be born of the descendants of the Pharaoh and of the queen — and so should he be given up unto your earth and to your people, and therefore, born with much wisdom.

And as thy have asked before of his beginning, for all these things shall come in fulfillment between your years of 1800 and 1999. But your earth shall change, for as we have said before, not one pebble upon your earth shall be left unturned.

[Note: Remember Jesus words, "But of that day and hour no one knows, not even the angels in heaven, nor the Son, but only the Father." (*Mark* 13:32)

For the fuse is lit from France to Israel. Unless the steps that are taken and the Eagle should protect unto the same, your earth shall be woven into blood of the same.

Pharaoh Akhenaten and Queen Nefertit sit in attendance as the rays from the one God shine upon and enter into them. The Pharaoh changed his name to Akhe-n-aten, meaning one who is useful to God. Through him, the rays from God entered and spoke. He was the first in Egypt to worship one God.

And as we have seen into your minds and souls, therefore, we should say unto this one, of [11–31–71–001], give praise unto your Lord that we may enter, that we may plant new knowledge before thee....

And we should say unto thee into these words. And we should make of this knowledge unto the one known as W___H____.

If thy know not where thy have been, thy should not know from where thy are going.

John the Baptist

As was done unto the one known as Moses, for as these people knew that
they had been in Egypt, and therefore, the Lord did say unto them, "We

shall deliver thee unto the promised land of the same," and as Moses did not enter, but therefore, was taken up into God to be held in His gentle arms — and as was said unto the one known as John the Baptist, "For was he not of Isaiah and Moses and of all mankind before him?" Was he not sent, therefore, to prepare a way for the coming of the Messiah?

Yet, do you denounce and deny these words?

And we say unto thee in this manner.

We are here but for one purpose, for the coming of the Messiah, for we reach outward for the need of your souls, to prepare a way upon your earth for this time.

[See *Exodus* 3:1–18, 12:14, 13:21–22, 14:15–20, 20:1–21, 33:5–23, 34:1–35, 36:8–9, 37:1–24, 40:34–38, *Deuteronomy* 31:9, 24–27, 34:1–5, and *John* 1:1–34.]

And as we have said before,

he has been born upon your earth. And as the Lord has sent him into the desert to be guarded, the time grows nearer. Must our Lord take him back to protect him? Or will thee stretch out thy arms and prepare a way within thyself?

[See *The Revelation*, chapter 12.]...

We should say unto thee — now is the time of the Cherub. [See *Genesis* 3:23–24, *Exodus* 13:21–22, 14:19–20, 33:7–11, 34:28–35, 36:8–9, 37:8–9, 40:34–38, and *The Revelation* 14:1–16, 19:1–16, 19:4–6, chapters 21–22.]

Cherub

December 10, 1971: We see thy need, and therefore, should say *again* unto thee these words. We have said before, do not misinterpret our words, and we have told thee that we have come but for one purpose, that purpose is to prepare a way for the coming of the Messiah.

We have said before to close your doors to no one, for all shall receive something, and if they are capable of shedding but one teardrop, this is enough.

But for those who should come to cause chaos and destruction into the same — before, thy have destroyed [thy prophets] and the prophets that came before, but this shall not be done. We shall allow no one in any form, either that that walks upon the earth in the form of the human animal, or that that walks in spiritual life, to interfere with this work. Therefore, we say unto thee these words. If thy have a stone to cast, let *us* stand before thee, and therefore, cast the first stone at us. This should be forgiven. But cast a stone at God, and this *shall not be* forgiven....

Therefore, we say unto those who should either harm *one member* of this group, beware, for the wrath of the Lord is mighty....

Thy have spoke of the words of philosophy and their meaning. There is only one philosophy, and that is truth. As has been said before, upon this rock we shall build a mighty kingdom for God. And from this rock shall flow a brook. And from the brook shall flow a river, and from the river shall flow many oceans to the many lands, to the many galaxies, to the many universes.

But it must be given with love, love for all mankind.

"My Father has many mansions." [See *John* 14:2.]

Remember, you can destroy nothing. Build upon what is already there. Give unto those who should receive with love and understanding. If they reject this, go to another, but take back your blessings. And give it again. If it is received, then take their blessings and learn of them, that [they] may learn of yours. Fear not the wrath of man, for man shall not harm one hair of the children of God, for not one sparrow may fall upon your earth without the permission of our Father. [See *Luke* 12:22–31.]

But remember also, there is a time for laughter, there is a time for work, there is a time for sleeping and rest, and there is a time to worship your God, each in his own way. For God has not made rules for the worship of Himself; man has done this.

He asks but two things, love of Him one-tenth unto the love He gives to His children; love of your fellow man in the same manner.

December 17, 1971: Yes, we see thy need. Therefore, we should say to thee these words. For as thy reach the time of year that thy should celebrate the birth, [as] the one known as Jesus Christ, we should say unto thee these words.

For as a gift was given once before, so it should be again.

But we should tell thee of the words and of the birth. For as we have said before, for God gave of His first-begotten son. And as He did give of Adam, so He begot of the same into this one known as Jesus. And yet, he did say unto man, "For [a] man to know of heaven, so he should know of earth."

Then we say unto thee, hark, and get these words.

For the wise to listen, let them listen. For the wise to see, let the see.

[See *Isaiah* 42:6–9, 18–21, 43:5–10.]

For as we have said before, we have come not to prove to you that we are great. We are but the servants of God.

And as it was so in another time, we did come upon the earth and prepare a way for the coming of [the] Messiah, and this we do again unto mankind.

But as your time is a different time, so it should be done in a different way. But the glory of God upon your earth shall be the same.

For He says to His children, "HARK, AND PREPARE A WAY THAT I MAY REST MY HEAD UPON YOUR EARTH." [See *Luke* 3:3–6, *Isaiah* 40:3–11, 11:1–10.]

Then we say unto thee –

as the time grows near when you should celebrate the birth of a before time, prepare that way within thy hearts and souls.

Prepare the way, that as before when he walked by the sea of Galliah [Galilee], and therefore, called unto his brothers, and they did come and walk with him — and as he did say unto them, "Come and I should teach thee to catch men," and so it was. [See *Mark* 1:14–20.]

But he brought unto this Earth love for all, for he could not see the difference in man's skin, for he looked only into their souls.

And as he came in five places upon your earth, it shall not be again. But he should come unto all races as one. And as he should love of all, so should man love of all.

And as once before, your planetary system was posed to give forth the light of a birth of a savior unto your earth, so it shall be again.

But we say unto thee, thy can destroy nothing. Therefore, build upon what exists of the same. It is not necessary that a man should call himself a Christian. It is not necessary that he call himself Mohammed, Ishmael. Nay, these are not important. It is what is in his heart, his true love for his God. These are the things that shall be counted.

And therefore, we say unto thee, as thy celebrate the birth, stand below the cross and count the drops of blood unto the same, and thy shall know the true meaning of this word you call love.

But be not sad. Rejoice unto the same, for thy Lord has not forgotten thee –

for this day shall come again. Then let your teardrops flow with joy unto the Lord.

Thy have many questions, ask.

"Yes, Aka. You spoke of the Star of Bethlehem, I believe. When the Messiah comes, will it be at the time that this star comes again, about 1998?"

Yes, we see thy need.

And if all is in preparation for the same, and if we have accomplished our mission upon your earth, then all shall be in readiness.

If we do not accomplish, then there shall be 300 years of darkness and bloodshed upon your earth. For remember, the last shall be first....

Yes, we see thy need. And therefore, we should answer in this manner.

For as we have said before, upon this rock shall flow a brook, and this brook shall be as the spirits of God — and from this brook should flow a

river, and this river should be as the spirits of man — and from this river should flow an ocean, that should be as the souls of man. But remember, God's spirit flows through all, and therefore, flows through all the lands, all the universes, all your galaxies.

But as we have said before, there shall be many who should not have but coin enough to buy but one loaf of bread. Let them buy of it, and pray upon the same, and we should turn thy water into wine, and we should make of thy bread into yeast, and therefore, should feed the multitudes of the same.

All thy must possess is the faith of God.

And the faith, if it be so small into the smallest creature of thy earth, this should be answered.

The 1972 messages on Preparing for the Coming

January 7, 1972: But we say unto thee, do not confuse this one thy call of Jesus with God, for he is the son of God, but he is not God. And as a good son should, he does give servitude unto his Father, and glory unto the same.

It is wise unto thee to ask, "For is this one, Jesus, as thy would know him, should serve as a priest of the high priest of [Manacok] [Melchizadek] for all time?"

But we should say unto thee, we are here to prepare a way.

We are here to prepare the way for the coming of the Messiah, and the Messiah shall be as a servant unto his Father.

Then live each day of thy lives and await his coming. For as he called thee before, he shall call thee again.

January 21, 1972: But we should say unto thee once again, we are not great. We are here as instruments of our Father. We are here but for one purpose, to prepare the way for the coming of the Messiah.

And we should say unto thee, this should take many hands, and much love and tenderness.

And we offer thee thy wine. If thy should decide to drink of the same, and therefore, become one of the many that stand before God, then we should speak unto thee at a different time. We may answer *all* of your questions that we are given permission to do so.

January 23, 1972: We see of thy other needs, and these things shall be provided, for as we have said before, we shall allow no one from either side to interfere with this work.

For we are here to prepare a way for the coming of the Messiah, and this, in itself, is the preparation of both your soul, your spirit and the immortal body of the same.

Do not act in haste. And beware of the dragons that stand near thee. But fear not, for the Lord, our God, walks with thee.

January 28, 1972: And now we should say unto thee these words. The time grows near when those of thy group thy have chosen for the ministry shall walk before our prophet, and therefore, be made unto ministers of this, our Father's work. And they should do so in this manner. Each should walk before this one.

And this one should say unto them, "Should thee promise in our Father's light to teach these things our Father has given unto thee to teach?

"Should thee at no time be prejudiced against any man?

"Should thee at all time, for those who come in need, minister in both healing of the body and healing of the soul and the spirit, and the immortal body of the same?"

And should they say, "yes," then he should take of what thy should know of the candelabra, but this one should have of seven candles. And each one who is chosen should be presented with this. And, as each time he should say, "yes," one candle should be lit. And then unto another.

These who should be chosen should be versed into the words we have spoken unto thee. They should have the honest effort unto helping mankind. And above all, they should enter all things with an open mind, closing their mind to nothing. And they shall never cease in their learning.

But you should remind them that the oath that they should take should be for [their] lifetime upon this plane and all others.

And then thy should ask into them, "Are you prepared to prepare a way for the coming of the Messiah?"

And should they say, "yes," then have them rise. And walk with them, and break bread with them and drink wine with them. For remember, for those who you shall choose, among you, nothing can be hidden from one another. All things must come in truth from God, for you shall walk in the light of God, and should be known as men and women of God....

Remember unto our words. Prepare you questions. Think deeply of the knowledge that thy should use, for the questions thy should ask and the answers thy should receive shall be passed on unto mankind. Make them wise.

[And] we should say unto the youth of your group, fear not that thy should prepare a way for the coming of the Messiah. Thy have many questions; ask of these. For did our Father not say unto thee, "BLESSED ARE ALL MY CHILDREN."

Now is the time of the Cherub.

February 4, 1972: Thy have other questions, ask.

"Yes, Aka. Is the Messiah to come the reincarnation of Jesus?"

When the proper time comes, our Lord should make this, His plan, known unto us, and we should tell of thee this.

But remember this, we can tell of thee nothing that our Lord, our God, our Father does not give unto us permission to do of the same. For our knowledge comes from Him who should know of all things.

February 11, 1972: Thy have many questions, ask.

"Aka, you have spoken of the Fifth Angel upon our earth. Are you speaking of the Fifth Angel as spoken of in Revelation, and what does this angel symbolize?"

Yes, we see thy need, and therefore, we should answer in this manner. As we have said before, your books of your Bible, both of the old and the new, are the records of very psychic people, those chosen to receive the words of God. But as they have beenhanded down from generation to generation, they have been added to and taken from.

Your book of Revelations, this should make the second happening of the same.

For once before, there stood a nation much like your own. At that time it was called the Roman Empire. And as it did fare before mankind, in the same manner, so should your own.

And the Fifth Angel unto which we speak should be of great disease, should be the opposite side of the great Sword, that which cuts land and masses, that which cuts into the souls and spirits of man, and therefore, changes them. All things that have been before shall be again. As Atlantis rose and so it fell beneath your seas, so it should be again. [See *The Revelation* 6:7–11.]

But we warn thee,

> *the time shall come, as has been promised, of a thousand years of peace upon your earth. But it shall not come before the great destruction comes upon your earth.*

[See *The Revelation* 20:1–6.]

In our kind, we have come to prepare a way for the coming of the Messiah.

And as we have spoke of the passing between the two world, for there is [are] many who should pass who do not understand and are not in the position to go forth into the temple of wisdom, the temples of learning.

> *And therefore, as you have read of the army of Armageddon, and prepare there, both upon heaven and earth for His coming, all these things must come to pass.*

[See *The Revelation*, chapter 19.]

Angel of Revelation

As we have said before, no man can harm your soul or your spirit. Our Lord has given unto thee free choice. Only you yourselves may do this.

And in this manner, you shall prepare a way for the coming of the Messiah.

You have thought in your own mind, "Should he come today, they would stone him." Nay. For as we have said before, a way shall be prepared, and no harm should come to this one.

For your world shall receive him in [holy bless], for upon his coming, not one soul shall remain who shall not bow before the Lord, Christ. For as we have said before, your Jewish nation shall bow before him.

But remember unto these words. The Jewish people were the chosen; they were chosen unto be the servants of our God. And as He did give them a coveth, so it was good in God's eyes, and as in the time of the one known as Jesus, Christ, did say unto thee, he had come to prepare a way. He had come not to change the prophecies, not to change the Law, but to show you the fulfillment of the same.

We realize there were times when we should speak as in riddles. But you should exercise your own wisdom by study.

And only in this manner can we prepare this way for yourselves.

February 25, 1972:

And we shall tell thee again of the seven spirits of your Father, and of the coming of the Messiah unto the same, for as we have said before, we were sent by those who should ask our Father to prepare a way for their coming.

And as man did come into five places upon your earth in the beginning, so it should be unto the five spirits that should enter at the time of the coming of the Messiah into the same, *for he shall not be of one spirit, but he should stand as the five of before. And as the seven spirits of our Lord shall descend into the same, and so it shall be again, the twelve shall walk upon your earth. And then, our Lord, God, should enter into this one and it should be of Thirteen.*

[See *Acts* 1:6–20, 2:2–28, *The Revelation* 1:4–9, 12–20, 4:1–6, and 12:1–2,10.]

As we have said before, the chain has been broken many times by your people through your foolish acts unto the same. But none should harm this one who should enter, for our Lord, God, shall be present in this one. And then should come your thousand years of peace upon the earth, and each day shall be as a thousand of your years, for they shall not be as you count, but as our Father counts. [See *The Revelation* 19:11–16, 20:1–6, 21:1–7, 22–26, and 22:3–7, 12–14, 16–17, 20–21.]

And as we have said before, the Hebrew people should bow before this one, for they should know that this is their Messiah in truth. [See *Isaiah*, chapters 11 and 52, *Zechariah,* chapters 12–14, and *The Revelation* 14:1–15 and 15:1–4.]

For as we have said before, Lord of Isaiah, Lord of Moses, Lord of Jesus, Lord of Buddha, Lord of Mohammed, Lord of Ishmael, so it should be again.

And we say, hark into thee, for as the first coveth [covenant] was given unto the Jewish people, and they, in themselves, were the servants of God, and as the second coveth was given unto the one known as Jesus Christ, so it has been in many lands, in many tongues, for as the spirit has flown and walked upon your earth. But remember unto these words. The coveth that was given unto the one known as Jesus was given not for the Jewish people, for they themselves had found their God; this was given that it may be given unto the world of the same. And as the coveth was given into Buddha, this was given that that proportion of your world should know of him. And as it was given unto Mohammed, it was given that they should know of the Jewish God, of the Jesus God, and of your God.

And now, we say unto thee again, we have come to prepare a way, and therefore, give unto thee a new coveth, and this coveth shall go unto the world. But remember these words — thy can destroy nothing; thy must build upon what is already there.

The sphinx or cherub was shown with wings in the centuries that followed after God led His people out from Egypt. The cherub is the throne bearer of God, Whose throne is upon the cherub's head.

And as we have said before, and the bird of the Great Pyramid shall, therefore, take wings again. [See *Exodus* 13:17–22, 14:18–24, 16:9–12.]

March 3, 1972: Yes, we see thy need, and therefore, we should say unto thee in these words. Thy have asked before, from whence we came? And we shall say unto thee in this manner. As soul Ray was reborn, and in this manner, so were we, for as has been said before, soul Ray is I and I is he. For as he prayed into his Lord for death, and this was given, but as he looked back upon his body, and looked into our Lord's eyes and knew that with the gift that was given he should return and give it unto others, but he had to give it in this manner, with love, with compassion at all times. This word you use so often, yet know so little about, this small word of yours, love, you cannot give it unless it is done freely. For, in giving this, each step that thy take thy grow closer unto our Father. Can you understand of which we speak? Nay, not fully. But the day shall come that thy shall. And we speak these words not only unto the disciples that we have named, for we name you all disciples before God.

But remember these words, we shall allow nothing or no one from either side of the curtain to interfere with this work, for it is far too important. We have given unto thee, as our Father has done unto all mankind, free choice. But we also have given unto thy keeping a prophet, a man who should stand before God, as he stands before you.

Thy have asked in thy mind, "Who should minister in your baptism, and who should minister in the sermons that are performed to each new minister?" This shall be done through your prophet. We have worked long and hard to prepare a way for the coming of the Messiah. And so shall you all.

Thy have asked in your minds, "What are these who speak to us?" And we shall answer in this manner.

For those of the spirits who should enter and become one, and therefore, become your Messiah and ours, have asked into our Lord to send those who stood beside them before, to prepare a way.

[See *John* 13:20, 14:15–21, 16:6–15, and 17:17–26, *Matthew* 17:1–13 and *Luke* 9:28–36.]

And we chose this one thy call thy prophet to [walk], work through, as once before in the one thy know as John the Baptist. [See *John* 1:6–34.]

Give praise unto thy Lord, thy God, and our Lord, your Father, your God shall give praise unto His children, and they shall become mighty both in heaven and earth. But remember, no man shall know of heaven that does not know of earth, and no man shall know of earth that does not know of heaven. [See *John* 1:6–34.]

But we say, hark, unto thee.

> *Why should you believe the words we speak of your earthly things and not believe these things we speak unto thee of heaven, as thy would call it?*

And they say, you say unto us, "What are these who speak in this manner? Are they angels? Are they archangels?"

And we should say unto thee, these are words of your own.

But we should answer in this manner.

> *We stand in pure light before our Father and you. We have found it necessary to speak in your tongue, of your language.*

But go forward; bear this yoke of love, and our Father shall reward into each of thee in thy own way.

March 10, 1972 [said to one person]: But as you have chosen to come as the time is made ready for the coming of the Messiah, so should our Father see fit to stay the hand, and therefore, let your learning grow greater into the same — and we say unto thee, [*kay-la-nos*], or brother of [love], for thy sight shall grow strong in the eyes of man and in the eyes of God. But wander no farther.

March 17, 1972: *"Thank you, Aka. [5-7-71-002] has asked if the infant Messiah of which you have spoken, 'Is it born already, as we understand it, and in what country?'"*

And we should answer in this manner. These things are known only unto our Father. And for, at the present time, for his protection, the exact location shall be kept a secret into the same.

But we should answer in this manner.

"Our Lord says, 'HARK,' into thee,

'For in the desert dwells, and therefore, by the sea,

Where the stars at night are seen all in 13 and more than 3.'

For the wise to hear let them hear. And for the wise to see let them see.

And when the time comes and the mountains bellow their mighty force –

our Father shall write upon the sky the entry of the same."

March 24, 1972: Yes, we see thy need, and therefore, should say unto thee in these words. There shall be rain, but not before the 24th day, of your time, of June, and this shall be slight. Thy shall have slight moisture from the Gulf of California. For the land shall become bare again.

But we shall say unto thee in this manner. As we have said before, this, in itself, can be changed; for as a group, through thy prayer this can be changed. Bring thy group together, and give forth in thy prayer for the same.

Yes, we see thy need, soul Luke, and we should answer your question in this manner.

For there is nothing to fear, but fear in itself,

for as we have said before, we shall allow no one from either side to interfere with this work. And as the time for the crow [cock] to crow is over, let thy groups stand fast together as the children of God. Send into thy enemies good thoughts, and leave thy trust in thy Lord, thy God.

And for those who should oppose the coming of the Messiah, as stones they shall be cast aside, as Lot, and risen again from the sea — for as the daughters of Lot walked forward and did sanctify Abraham, and as God saw it was good and gave blessings upon the same. [See *Genesis* 18:16–33, 19:2–29, and *The Revelation* 20:11–15.]

April 1, 1972: *"Yes, Aka. [4-1-72-001] who is here with us tonight has asked for direction. And she would also like a health or life reading."*

We shall answer first in this manner. We have come but for one purpose, that, in itself, is a preparing of a way for the coming of the Messiah. If thy should take unto thyself this purpose, carry the torch before thee and light the way for others. We shall enter and give thee guidance....

And now we say unto thee these words. For those who should see us, for those who should see us materialize in human form, we should answer your question in this manner.

For those who have seen us have seen our Father, for we stand before Him as servants. We are here to prepare the way for the coming of the Messiah. Glory be His name.

Go out among your people. Give them your message, and we shall go with thee.

But the time grows short, for the Fifth Angel lies upon thy earth, and beside him *stand* four more. There is but two to pass before thee, and pray that these seals are never opened. [See *The Revelation of John* 6:1–11.]

Give us but one soul in each of what thy know as thy towns, and we shall spare of this in our Father's day.

April 14, 1972: And we should say unto thee these words, soul James, for thy have asked these words of communion into the same. And we should answer you in this manner. We are here to prepare the way for the coming of the Messiah. We do not ask from any of you other than the love of your God — and as we have said before, our Father has many mansions; therefore, you can destroy nothing, but you may build on what is already there.

We have told into thee to take [up, of] the bread and the wine, for the bread shall be your soul and spirit, and the wine shall be that of our Father's — for as the body, the soul, and the spirit should come in completion of the immortal body of the same.

And they asked of the wine. Place of this before each. If they chose to, let them partake of the same.

But our Father does not ask for the blood of the Lamb. And the Lamb does not ask for the blood of man. For these things that belong to the earth also belong to our Father, for they were His in the beginning. And should the grape choose to become the wine for your offering, then the grape has seen fit to use of its free choice.

And should the wheat of thy bread choose to come forth of its free choice unto your offering — and should our Father's children see to come forth of their free choice, and therefore, give up into our Father the offering of the same, this is their choice.

But remember, this can be done anywhere, for this is between them and their God.

But as you should become ministers in the light of God, and therefore, speak of the words of God, this can be done unto your own people and those with free choice who come unto thee and ask.

But as we have said before, go unto this house and knock. If they should bid you enter, drink of their wine, that they may drink of yours. But should they not, then take of this, and go elsewhere.

But we should say unto all of the disciples of this work, give that that is God's to God; give that to your brother that is your brother's; but just as important, give that unto yourselves that is yourselves'. But close your doors to no man.

For we do not come to one people alone, but to all the people and all the children of God. Therefore, give glory unto God and God should give glory unto His children.

But mark these words — for those who have been chosen to walk in the light of God and minister in the same manner, walk as a man and a woman of God. Be as a mirror into the same. For as we have said unto thee, *for those who should see us should see of our Father, and thine should be likewise in the same manner.*

Do not step backwards....

Thy have come, for thy are in need again to prepare a way for the coming of the Messiah. We should leave unto thee this knowledge. Dwell at it. And come and ask again, and we shall [bid, give] thee farther in thy wisdom.

We can see in thy mind much confusion. But open the door, that we may enter....

But we leave unto all of thee these words. For the teacher should feel great and mighty in the eyes of man, but within their hearts, if they should stay humble in the eyes of God — and God shall make them great.

But a student shall never become more than the teacher, and the teacher shall never become more than the pupil.

But your time of learning has come forth, and the Great Pyramid and the bird of the Great Pyramid should take flight, for now we shall give of thee the powers thy ask for.

April 17, 1972: Thy have other questions, ask.

"Yes Aka. [2-19-71-002] of...[Amperhand] Ave., Apt ____, Yonkers, New York, has had a dream in which she saw two birds flying in the sky, and they came down and sat on a fence and sang beautiful songs and then flew away leaving some feathers. She would like to know the meaning of it."

The spiritual messengers of God looked into the dream, saw what would be, and spoke sadly: Yes, we see thy need, and we should answer in this way. Though where thy dwell shall be destroyed, it shall come again. And all shall come in peace before this one thy should know as the Christ, for, as we have said before, we come but for one purpose and that is in the preparation for the coming of the Messiah. Can thy understand of which we speak?

"No, Aka, I cannot."

Then give it thought into the same, and the answer shall dwell within thy souls.

Editor's note: In this message 30 years beforehand, did the spiritual messengers of God foresee what would happen on September 11, 2001 — that two airplanes would destroy the twin towers of the World Trade Center — as they answered this question April 17, 1972, of a woman from New York about her dream?

April 21, 1972: And we say hark into thee. For as we have said before, now is the time of the Cherub. And the Fifth Angel rests no longer upon thy earth, for *now* is the time of the great Sword that should cut of land and masses.

And we shall say once again that your earth is slowly changing upon its own axis. But your earth is sliding with this change. It has done this many times before.

But this time it should be done with purpose, that mankind may hear and heed the words of God.

Our Lord has given unto thee free choice. But yet, you go onward with your wars and your killing. And we say unto thee, our Father does not seek the blood of the Lamb, but gave it to you that thy may see for thyselves in the resurrection of your own. Yet you took this and misinterpreted these words, and misinterpreted the deed within itself.

And now, as we have said before, your earth, this planet of yours, shall show that it has karma too. For earthquakes should come within your land. The earth should heave and give forth unto new life. And the temple of God that is in within man shall shine forth, and come again.

And thy ask unto thyselves, "Why do they talk in riddles?" [Yet] we have given unto thee many words. We have given unto thee many lessons to pass forth upon the people of the land.

We do not come to you alone. We have chosen you first to prepare a way for the coming of the Messiah.

But first you must prepare the way within yourselves.

April 28, 1972: Yet we come but for one purpose — that in itself is the preparation for the coming of the Messiah.

And we come with love. But we also come from the One we were sent.

And our Father should shed many tears for His children.

June 2, 1972: We have said before, do not misinterpret our words; do not twist them to meet your own selfish needs, and this has been done. And we should say unto thee, beware, for the wrath of the Lord is great, for nothing from either side shall be allowed to interfere with this work.

We are here but for one purpose, and that is in the preparation for the coming of the Messiah. And those who are chosen should prepare first within themselves.

If they cannot do this, let them walk away. We have asked you to promise nothing. Those things that thy gave unto thy Lord was given of thy free will.

We have asked but two things –

to love unto thy Lord one-tenth of the love the Lord should give unto thee, to love unto mankind in the same manner, and to coveth nothing that should belong to another.

And for those who should encourage this, then they should walk alone and become lost souls. And we should say unto thee these words, the Lord giveth and the Lord taketh away, for not one stone upon your Earth may be moved without His knowledge and His consent....

And we should say to those who should walk away, all thy must do is open the door that we may enter, for we are not great; we are but the servants and messengers of your Lord, God.

But we have given unto thy hands a prophet. Beware, those who should stone him. Beware, those who should cast false accusations unto the same. Your Lord, your Father, is a loving Father. He should give love and kindness unto all. He has given unto thy keeping free will, but only that thy should not violate another's free will.

June 14, 1972: *"Yes, Aka, my nephew [6-16-72-002] has written me a letter, and he feels that he has a special calling and mission, and that he is being directed in some direction that has to do with God which he does not yet understand. And I have been asked, he's asked me to write him back and give him my thoughts, and can you give me counsel for him?"*

Yes, we should answer in this manner. As the prayers were given unto our Father, so they were answered. As the guidance was given unto our Father, so this was answered.

Temptation shall be cast before this one. And we should answer in this manner. If this, now, is what thy desire, if the debt that thy should pay should be in full,

prepare then thyself, within thyself, for the coming of the Messiah.

Venture forth unto this land.

And now, we shall give unto thee the bread and the wine. But this must be done of your own free will.

So far, we have given unto this one the guidance that was needed. For, as we have said before, as our Father and the spirits of God should be as a brook, as the spirits of man should be as a river, as the souls of man should be as a vast ocean, all should come unto the many lands.

We shall say in this manner, we have reached and touched unto many lands. Many shall venture forward to taste of this wine, that it shall grow.

And we shall unto you, soul Paul, prepare of that within thyself, for now, that that should reach the many lands shall come into fulfillment, for light shall be shown unto all who should venture outward. Encourage soul Ray to now <u>use of the radio</u> <u>communications in all respects to broaden the</u> <u>knowing of the people of himself and</u> <u>the work.</u>

Now is the time of the Cherub; now is the time of the preparation for His coming.

Oh Lord, oh Lord, Almighty of all. Oh man, oh man, almighty of all, bow before these who should make their presence known, for they should come of the spirit of our Father, yet each of a separate part, but into one. Place upon your Earth that that should be in man.

Save of the many religions upon your Earth. Give feast unto all.

Praise and glory shall come from our Father. And those who should give glory unto our Father, glory shall be unto man of the same.
June 16, 1972: Yes, we see thy need and we should answer in this manner.

As the flowers were given upon your Earth to show you the beauty that lay within man's soul, as the gift of love is given unto mankind, not once, but many times from your Father —

and as your world came apart from itself and, therefore, joined unto the mighty universe and universes of the vast planetary system, and that, within itself, became part of your Father, each of you in your own way have reached to the heavens and touched them. Each of you in your own way, for only a moment, have opened your hearts and souls, and felt the love that is given by our Father.

But so often you should pull away from Him, and therefore, become lonely and alone.

As a man and woman should join be joined before God in matrimony, and therefore, give of their love unto one another, therefore, they should feel within themselves a touch of God, a touch of the creating power which lays upon your Earth. This same power was given unto the smallest.

Yet, into man it was given unto the mightiest of all, sometimes in a simple form, [some others] in mighty forms. Throughout the plane of man there have been many who have touched the psychic world and returned. There have been many who could not return. Yet, few of these were looked upon by mankind with love and kindness. They were set apart, apart from others, and separated.

We have said before that the sons of man and the sons of God were of much the same in making. But we should say, now, that as the sons of God did look upon the daughters of man and find them fair, and therefore, did enter, and lose their way, and therefore, could not return, all of mankind, even into the smallest animal, this psychic power was given. [*Genesis* 5:1–32, 6:1–4]

But unto the sons of God it was never forgotten, and therefore, the descendants and the descendants of the same have come forth upon your earth with far memory, memory of the psychic abilities they possessed in each lifetime. And yet, as in that time, they were set aside, and the man-animal became afraid of them, and did destroyed them....

And we should say again unto thee these words. Destroy not the prophets that we have placed upon your earth, for they shall be the gateway unto your God, for so it was written in the beginning. But measure your prophets in this manner.

If that that they have given unto you is true, and truths, then accept this as a gift from God.

But if that which they have given unto you is false, and not true, and should not stir that memory within thyselves of thy Father, then walk away from these, for they are not prophets. And so it was written in the beginning, and so it shall be.

Thy have many questions, ask of the same....

From a past-life reading, Aka tells of one who felt the drops of blood and guides this one of the preparation for the coming of the Messiah in this time:

And thy Father said, "GO UNTO THE MOUNT OF THE SKULL AND WAIT."

And so thy did. And of that morn thy saw of the ointed One come forward. And thy stood and watched as the hands and feet were staked unto the cross. And thy walked forward and bent in prayer and in humbleness. But as thy walked forward, one drop of blood fell upon thy forehead, and thy looked up and knew what God had said, that it was not an ending, but a beginning of the same.

Many miles and many lives thy have lived since this time. But remember, thy were chosen to count the drops of blood, and thy were chosen to carry One forever. Thy should reach upon thy forehead, and therefore, should feel the love that was given unto your Father that day.

[Spoken to one]: But as we have said before, we have come, not to make mankind great in the eyes of other men.

We have come once again that those drops of blood should not be spilt in vain. We have come to prepare the way for the coming of the Messiah.

Therefore, reach unto thy forehead, for it shall be there. Prepare that way within thyself as before. For now we have returned first one [the prophet] unto thy keeping, and soon another [the Messiah].

But this time there shall be no dungeon. This time there shall be no crucifixion.

If what we have done and the time that we should have left to prepare this is used well by all, mankind shall rise above himself,

and when the coming, that that shall be written in the sky, is felt in full, then all of mankind shall feel truth and humbleness.

And upon your earth shall dwell a thousand years of peace, but not as you count, but as our Father counts.

But remember, those thousand years shall be different unto each one. Your years of peace could start at this moment.

Find that peace within yourself, that love that was given within this drop of blood, and return it into your fellow man in the manner that it was given.

We know thy do not understand fully these things we have given unto your keeping, but thy shall. For as before, thy reached and sought for the meaning of true love, and our Father spoke unto thee, so He shall once again. Thy life has not been in vain, for once again those thy dwelt with thy dwell again. And so it shall be again.

June 23, 1972: For we have spoke before of the Fifth Angel upon thy earth. And as we have spoken unto thee of this great Sword, the mighty Sword that cuts two ways, therefore, we should speak again of these things. And we should say unto thee,

where no water flowed, water shall flow, that the clouds shall open unto abundance of the same. And this, in itself, shall be the first sign,

for as he walks upon your earth, that that thy have built shall be destroyed, that that thy have placed within the ocean shall rise and poison man.

Yea, yea, we say unto thee these words. For those who have been written in the beginning, their names shall be taken a poll unto the same, And our Lord, God, should give unto them guidance and peace of mind, and the gift of life shall be given unto those.

But for those who should walk away and turn their backs unto God, and should serve unto Lucifer, they shall be cast aside. [See *The Revelation*, chapters 6 and 20.]

For as we have said before, we shall walk before thee, and therefore, the might of the Lord shall be present within thee.

Therefore, give unto the Lord that that is due unto Him. Give unto your fellow man that that is due unto him. But give unto yourself also that that is due unto you.

And we should say in this manner, proportions of your Earth shall now start to change. In some areas they shall come as a rapid thing. We have given warnings before, and thy have not listened unto our words.

For what was unclean shall be made clean again, for now is the time that the preparations shall be made for the coming of the Messiah.

For those who should walk in the light of God, no harm shall come unto those.

June 30, 1972: Yes, we see thy need, and we should answer in this manner, that is of of before time, when the Earth slowed in its axis, as we have told you before. And as the time that the Earth and your time stood still — and your Earth is now again reaching its same position, for as we have said before, not one stone upon your Earth shall be left unturned. [See *Matthew*, chapter 24.]

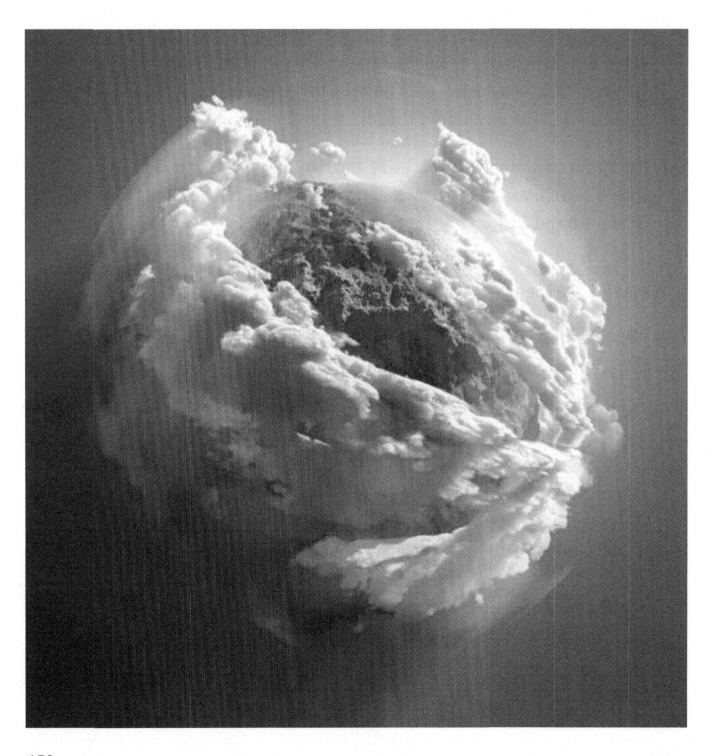

But we say unto thee, beware, for the Fifth Angel walks upon thy Earth.

But for the children of God, thy have nothing to fear, for we shall walk before thee and prepare a way.

We have come unto thee but for one purpose and that is for the preparation for the coming of the Messiah. We have given unto thee the keeping of the date and time. And of your year, 1998, so it shall be upon your Earth. [Remember that Jesus said, "But of that day and hour no one knows, not even the angels in heaven, nor the Son, but only the Father." (*Mark* 13:32)]

But first shall come the sign and the writing in the sky.

And we say unto thee in these words,

for all shall bow and pay homage into this One.

Yet, all shall be glad within their hearts, for your suffering upon the Earth shall end, and as has been promised, a new heaven and a new earth shall begin.

But we saw unto thee in these words,

as we have come to prepare this way, do so within thy own hearts and souls, that thy may serve the Messiah in the manner unto which your Lord, God, should wish of this, the same.

But first, proportions of your earth must be cleansed, and that that man has placed in the sea shall come forth and sting of them, as scorpions. And that that man should place in the earth should cause destruction and movement of the earth in the same manner. <u>We have told thee of the Amchitka zone and that of the destruction that</u> <u>would slowly come from this.</u> We have shown thee of many paths and many lessons. We have told thee before that before the destruction should come in any proportion, that this work should go forward. Warnings should be given in advance. And even though we have given warnings, some have not believed and had little faith, and therefore, were destroyed by their own lack of faith.

July 7, 1972: Now, we should say unto thee, we have come before thee but for one purpose, and that purpose is for the preparation for the coming of the Messiah. We have seen that that thy have done to develop thy own psychic abilities, and we have blended into thee the knowledge that was needed. We shall not take this away from any of you, but it shall remain.

August 11, 1972: And we should say unto thee again, let the dead bury their dead, for our Father should be the God of the living, not the dead. And for those who should dwell as lost souls, let them bury their dead also. For now shall be a new time. And we shall bring forth the knowledge that has hidden before.

And we shall tell thee of the time that shall come before thee in fulfillment, for as once before, as Judas should slay a Prophet, and the Prophet rose again, so it shall be in this time, for not until the Prophet was slain should the truth come in fulfillment. And as it was written, so it shall be.

And we shall say unto thee into these words, as we have said before.

Thy Father asks but two things of thee, love unto Him one-tenth the love given unto thy fellow man, love unto your Father in the same manner.

And we should say unto thee these words. Coveth not that that should belong to another. For we should answer your questions in this manner.

For the Lord of Isaiah, for the Lord of Abraham, for the Lord of Ishmael, for the Lord of Moses, and for the Lord of the one known as Jesus Christ, and so it shall be for the Lord of the one known as Buddha —

for they did not worship false idols, nor did they lay any idol or prophecy before themselves.

154

For the Lord came in truth unto man and gave unto him the Spirit, and the Lord should stand before thee in the same manner.

But man can harm thee, yes, this is true, but he cannot take from thee thy soul or thy spirit. Even your Lord, God, should not do unto this of thee. But He should allow thee to do it unto thyselves. If this in that manner has been done, then woe unto thee who had walked in a false light and given unto his fellow man lies, and not truths.

But now we should say unto thee these words, we have come but for one purpose, and that is the preparation for the coming of the Messiah.

Your earth, as we have said before, shall start to change.

Your changes shall come from Alaska, through the Mediterranean, through the Mexican and South Americans, and all land within the same shall mold and come forth. The land that should be of the Brittany shall change.

And the land that thy should know of the valley below the sea, it shall change, for it has changed in man's eyes already. [Note: the Yuma, Arizona, or Imperial Valley, California, area.]

Of this we say unto thee, your thousand years can begin at any time, but not as you should count, but as our Father should count.

And for some there shall be many, and for some there shall be never.

But the half times are over, for those who should pass beyond this time, they shall be. For those who should lose of their souls shall be no more, for they shall wander in nothingness.

August 26, 1972: Thy have other questions, ask.

"Thank you, Aka. [8–26–72–003], age nine, of Yuma...asks, 'I want to know what direction God wants me to take to build for the future.'"

We should answer in this manner.

For we have come but for one purpose, to prepare a way for the coming of the Messiah. This can only be done with an army of minds. This can only be done within each soul.

We have come to take from the brook into the rivers, from the rivers into the many lands, and unto the universes and universes, as the heavens themselves. [But as] each soul comes forward once again to take from that their karma — no one else can do this for them only they themselves — but if you should stop along the way to show the path unto others, then blessed be those who should give of the Light.

Go unto meditation, open thy mind, and therefore, the door shall be opened that we should enter, and we should give unto thee the knowledge that is needed....

But as a small child who suckles [its] mother, go unto the temple of God for knowledge, for none who should know not of heaven should not know of earth, for none who should not know of earth shall not know of heaven.

And we should say again, for the time grows near,

for written upon your sky, the earth shall bellow forth its mighty force.

And there, upon the desert it shall lie, close to the ocean, for within real –
but Satan, therefore, cannot steal.

[See *Matthew* 24:29–33, *Acts* 1:6–11, *The Revelation* 14:14, 19:11–16, and *The Revelation* 12:10–17.]...

And we say unto thee, the Fifth Angel walks upon your earth. Not one stone shall be left unturned. [See *The Revelation,* chapters 5–7 and *Matthew* 24:1–8.]

September 1, 1972: And we should say once again in this manner. Give unto your Lord glory, and your Lord should give unto thee glory in return. But, as in the days of David, so glory came from the earth and into the heaven and gave unto the people of Israel glory. [*I Samuel, 2 Samuel, 1 Kings.*]

But as in your days of Rome, as Rome gave glory into the Romans, so they fell upon the earth. And so it shall be once again. For those who should walk in the light of our Father, all things shall come unto past,

for as the Book of the beginning was so, so should the Book of the ending be of the same....

[From a life reading:] And now, as another time has come upon your earth, thy have chosen to return once again to see this time. Yet, within thy heart thy have not seen where thy have been, so therefore, thy have not chosen direction of where thy should go. And we say unto thee these words.

We have come but for one purpose, for the preparation of the coming of the Messiah, for no other reason.

And we say unto you, many souls have chosen to come again upon this earth for the same purpose. But even through their choice they must still choose to prepare the way within themselves, first.

Do this. Become as one, but yet, become as five. And walk before thy God and know what thy God said unto thee, "COME UPON THE EARTH, AND YET, BE FRUITFUL. GIVE UNTO THE HOUSE OF THE LORD THE CHILDREN THAT SHALL BE NEEDED FOR THIS TIME."

And this thy have not done. Thy have chosen to walk alone. Yet, we say unto you, take the doubt from thy mind and go forward in a just manner.

There are many lifetimes of thy past and which thy question, and thy wonder within thy mind why we have chosen just one to give unto thee. Yet, we should answer in this manner. If thy can learn from just this one, then thy should know within thy heart and soul of all the others.

We should give unto thee this. At another time we shall fulfill thy cup until it should runneth over, and thy should know of many lands and many places....

"Yes, Aka, [9-1-72-003] had two dreams that she would like to ask about. She asks, 'Can you explain about the baby I saw in meditation with the beast? And also the dream with the red door and the tiny lights in my room?'"

We should answer of your first question in this manner. For as the Messiah should come upon your earth, so should Lucifer stand near to gather from the mother's womb that which was placed upon the earth. Yet, this shall not be allowed. [*The Revelation* 12:1-17].

For as we have said before,

it shall be where the stars shall shine of brightness, where the sea shall be close at hand, and yet, the desert in itself shall coveth this one.

Therefore, if the way is prepared within thee and within others, this of the child shall not be taken back unto God and guarded, but shall be given unto mankind.

Go unto the readings of the before, and thy shall find the answer to the fulfillments of your last dream, and of your first.

September 8, 1972: Ask that in your meditation that we may enter, and we should come unto your mind, for as we have said before that as the spirits of God should flow as a brook, as the soul of man should flow as a river, as the souls of man should flow as an ocean, yet the spirit of man should flow through all.

Yet, not all of mankind that walks upon your earth should have of the spiritual form. Therefore, we should reach you into the many lands, and as you should be reached, so should others, so should the other knowledge that can be given. There are many of your kind in the land on which you dwell.

We are here but for one purpose, and that purpose is to prepare the way for the coming of a Messiah, and therefore, should build an army of minds, but first, the way must be prepared within yourself.

Pick your time each day for meditation — quite simply that pray unto God that the words of Aka may enter; therefore, by opening the door, we shall enter and make ourselves known unto you.

If thy should take of the wine, we should provide of the bread and the yeast, and therefore, thy cup should runneth over. We should await thy answer unto the same.

September 15, 1972: "And we should say unto thee, blessed be that that is brought unto our Lord, and blessed be that that is given from our Lord. And for those who should choose to walk in our Father's light, have they but one teardrop to shed, then all is in accord. But give that unto your Father that thy would give unto thyself. Give it in the same measure. For those who should walk alone, and be lonely, they shall never be alone, for our Father shall walk with them.

All they must do is open the door and we shall pass through unto the same....

"But we should say unto thee these words...there shall come upon your earth many changes of your seasons. And we shall provide for each of these. But as a tree should grow we have pruned this. Bear no one ill will, for only that that was done, was done at the will of our Father, which was written in the great Book should come in fulfillment. As we have said before, we are not great, we are but the messengers of our Father.

"Can you understand of which we speak? Nay, not fully.

Then we should say in this manner,

for all upon heaven and earth has been made in readiness.

Have faith, for we are here but for one purpose, and that is to prepare a way for the coming of a Messiah.

Have faith in your Father and He shall have faith in you. Give unto your Father glory and He should give it unto you. Give unto your Father love and He shall give it unto you. And the love of our Father shall be shown before all mankind, and proof shall be given of the same.

But give unto mankind glad tidings.

For though your earth's surface shall change, and though the Sword that should cut two ways shall be present, even in all of these things shall be the joy of His arrival upon your earth.

For has not our Father promised unto thee a new heaven and a new earth?

And so it shall be.

But prepare within thyselves the valley of our Lord.

September 22, 1972: And you should say unto us, "Why should you call this one a prophet, and no longer call of him an instrument?"

And we should answer in this manner. For we have placed within his mind, the awakening mind, the ability to see those things of the future clearly. For has it not been written that your Father should send unto one who could not be slain, and for those of the beast who should try to slay him, our Father would let him lie dormant and then rise him before the beast? [See *The Revelation* 11:1–13.]

And so it has been done. And the beast we speak of is the doubt and greed within the minds of many.

Yet, we say unto you, remember of these words. That we may continue using this one, his fulfillment as a man must be also in complete.

And you asked of his different moods. And we say unto you, as the wind should change and the leaves should blow, his mind should reach forth into the many areas of your world, and of your minds. But we did not bring this one forward in this manner to make him great in the eyes of men, for he did not desire this. He granted permission to be used, but only in this manner, for the preparation of the coming of the Messiah.

That that was done unto him has healed, but the scars are still new. Walk carefully upon them, for we have removed the block within his mind. And we should say unto you, nothing is hidden from his mind. This, in itself, he must become accustomed to. Before, he knew that he could not harm any person or thing upon your earth with his mind. But now he must govern it with his own conscience, and this, in itself, is a learning time within him. But fear him not, for his conscience shall walk with God.

October 13, 1972: And we should say unto these words.

First, we should say unto the one known as [5-7-71-002], walk as Matthew, and thy cup shall runneth over.

But we come not to promise thee the worldly needs, we come not to make thee great in the eyes of man, we come but for one purpose, that purpose is in the preparation for the coming of the Messiah.

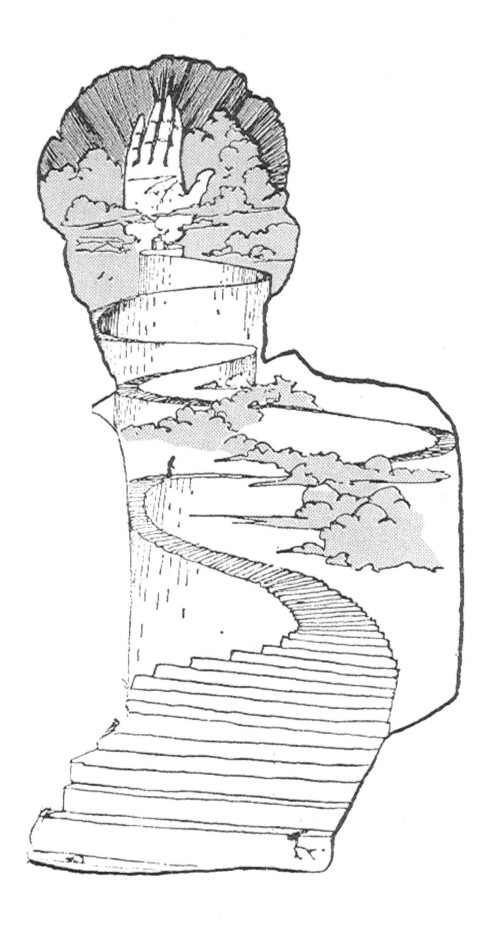

And we say these words unto you,

if thy should believe the earthly things, then thy should believe those things of our Father.

But if thy cannot believe of which we speak, there are many mansions and our Father shall provide one for you. Our Father has planted into your hands that of free choice. Neither ourselves or our Father shall take this from you. We have entered into thy house many times, for thy bid us welcome. We have placed unto thy hand our wine.

But we also placed unto all those who do the work of God a time of temptation, a time of doubt. We did this in this manner that the house of God could be cleansed.

For those who should walk in the light of our Lord and the work that is needed in the preparation for his coming shall have the strength to carry the mighty Sword, for now is you time of Armageddon.

[See *The Revelation*, chapter 19.]

For many doors unto your mankind shall be opened. Your radio and television media shall be placed before you. The hearts and minds of thousands and millions shall be placed into your hands.

But all those, one by one, and two by two, and three by three were to be tested. And those who could not stand should be cast aside. And those who shall not stand shall be cast aside. For is it not written that if thy right eye should offend thee cast it aside? For thy Lord, God, is a jealous God, and He shall have no other gods before Him, or after Him.

And for the one who should come shall not come as a god, but as a servant of God. Yet, he shall carry the spirits of God within him, and he shall carry within him that of the Christ-state of many.

Jesus transfigured on the mount (Matthew 17:1–11)

For he shall come as the first-born son of our Father.

For is it not written that our Father loved this world of yours and mankind that He should hand into your hands once before His first-begotten son who He loved very dearly. And is it not written that the descendants of Abraham should be changed as stones. For you shall serve one of your own kind.

Yet, as the spirit of God should dwell within you, so it should dwell within this one. But the power of God should also dwell within this one, and the wisdom and the love our Father has for His many children.

For if it was not so, our Father would have told you. For our Father has hidden nothing from His children. For what has been laid in darkness shall be placed into the light.
What was covered shall be uncovered.

For a new heaven and a new earth shall come and all things our Father has promised shall be as it was written.

[See *The Revelation,* chapters 21–22.]

For did not our Father promise that two prophets should come to the earth and they should be slain and risen again. And so it shall be.

And so it is, for have you not seen it with your own eyes? [See *The Revelation,* chapter 11.]

Yet, thy say, of the many, unto us, "Perform, therefore, a miracle, and we should believe."

And we say unto you, we have come not to perform miracles, as thy would know them, for we can do nothing without the permission of our Father, for it is not us who should give healing, but our Father.

It is not us who should show you light in the darkness, but our Father, for we are but the servants of our Father, and we walk in His holy light.

But those who should walk in our Father's light and give praise unto Him, of the Creator, the Father, the God, then light shall be shown forever and ever.

But we should also unto you these words, for those who should not believe, watch your earth tremble. Watch those who should not believe fall into the earth and be devoured by it, and yet live in fear. Watch those who have become so concerned with their selves that they have no room for God create their own hell and walk in nothingness.

Yet, you say unto us, then now is the time of sorrow. And we say. nay, you are but foolish children,

for now is the time of joy, and the joy should be in your hearts for the day of the preparation. For upon your earth shall be a thousand years of peace, but not as you count, but as our Father should count, and each day should be as a thousand years.

And your earth shall change its form. Where no water flow, water shall flow; what was desert shall be made into gardens.

Your times of trail are but a short time. This time of the Anti-Christ, that is short upon your earth to come, is but a short time. Yet, for those who should not show the mark of the Beast, all things unto our Father shall be given. [See *The Revelation*, chapters 12– 13, 14:8–12, and chapters 15, 17, and 19–22.]

And we say unto thee, give glory unto our Father, and our Father shall give glory unto you, and glory be the name of the Lord, our Father, forever and ever.

Let that of the light that was placed there in the beginning to see, open this, and let it see, and thy shall see us, and thy shall see thy Father. But deny thyselves, and thy shall see darkness....

And we should say unto soul [_], our Father has seen of thy needs. And thy shall walk with the children of God. Give patience unto thy Father, for what is a day in the time of glory and happiness? For thy Father has shown unto you love, has shown unto all of His descendants since the disciples that of love, for you all are the children of God.

And we say unto the disciples, prepare therefore a haven within thyselves of love. But remember, thy are shepherds; do not allow the wolves to attack thy sheep. Stand as David, and thy shall stand as the shepherd of people of God.

We see thy needs, soul Paul. We see that of the questions thy would ask.

The healing that is needed shall be given to those with faith in their hearts upon this night of nights.

Was this "night of nights," October 13, the eve when Jesus was born?

And therefore, we should say unto you, for we shall place in thy mind a prayer unto your Father, and before your meeting should end this night, thy should tell of the people of the same. Now is the time of the Cherub.

October 27, 1972: *"Yes, Aka. [5–7–71–002] also asks, 'On the seven candlesticks mentioned in Revelations, are they us and a reference to our bodies?'"* [See *The Revelation of John*, chapters 4–5.]

Yes, we see thy need. And these shall be, as we have said before, the Seven Spirits of God. But you must realize that that was before has happened already in the rise and fall of the Roman Empire.

Jesus Ascends to Heaven.

"Therefore, when they had come together, they asked Him, saying, 'Lord, will You at this time restore the kingdom to Israel?' And He said to them, "It is not for you to know times or seasons which the Father has put in His own authority. But you shall receive power when the Holy Spirit has come upon you; and you shall be witnesses to Me in Jerusalem, and in all Judea and Samaria, and to the end of the earth. Now when He had spoken these things, while they watched, He was taken up, and a cloud received Him out of their sight. And while they looked steadfastly toward heaven as He went up, behold, two men stood by them in white apparel, who also said, "Men of Galilee, why do you stand gazing up into heaven? This *same* Jesus, who was taken up from you into heaven, will so come in like manner as you saw Him go into heaven."'" (*Acts* 1:4-11)

As a Messiah did come of before, and a Messiah shall come once again, this should make your Revelations twofold.

December 1, 1972: Yes, we see thy need, and therefore, should say unto thee in these words, for as we have told you of the beginning, and as we have told you of the twin sisters of your earth, and therefore, we shall bring those forward into one house, that all may prepare for the coming of the Messiah.

For look deep within yourselves; bring forth that that belongs to your Father. Place it upon the altar.

But do not cast before an animal that that belongs to God, and do not cast an animal before your God, that that belongs to man. And thy say once again unto us that we speak in riddles. Yet, we say unto you, for the wise to hear, bring forth the altar of our Father. Lay it before you. Cast aside your animal instincts. Cast them aside and throw them to the winds. But remember, even that the wind should blow should be our Father's will. Bring forth that part of yourselves that was in the beginning. Place forth before our Father of pure kind....

What you do, now, is more important than that you have ever done before,

for all things that you have done before has brought you to this time, this place, now. Give forth our Book wings and let it fly unto the people.

And we say unto you, soul [1-21-72-002], we have placed flowers before you. But now is not the time for flowers, for now we have come to collect your indebtedness. And our Father shall collect it in full in this manner.

Universal Philosophy

Part 2 of 2
Spoken 1977–1989

The BOOK with Wings (Book 1)
by Aka, spiritual messengers of God

New words shall be written upon the sky,
but they must be written in men's hearts first.

Thy have the knowledge. Use of it.

And now, we say unto soul Paul these words, your debts shall now be brought before you. For all things that are promised unto our Father shall be fulfilled. Give healing unto those that are needed. Give guidance unto those that are needed. But yet, as we placed you, not third from the right, but first to the right, that you should stand as a pillar and give strength unto soul Ray, and bear the yoke.

And now, we say unto soul [5-7-72-004] these words. Come forth unto us as Mark. Come forth unto us in fullness, for the children should wait unto your coming. But as your promise of before, your time has arrived, and now our Father shall place before thee a way to repay your indebtedness.

And now, we say unto soul Luke these words. As we read from your records and your promises unto our Lord, we come before you, therefore, to collect this indebtedness to your God, your Father. You have made promises unto your Lord. Take forth this Book of Wings and spread it unto the nations of the earth.

And now we say unto soul James, those tools that are needed shall be placed in your hands. And as we read from your records of your indebtedness, we have come to collect of the same. Go forth and spread the words that are given unto you.

And now, we say unto soul Jude, your time is here, and now we have fulfilled our part of the bargains. We have saved and spared the life of your son. We have saved and spared the life of your grandchildren. We have saved and spared the life of your daughters and your husband. Now is the time our Father should collect that that is owed unto Him.

But yet, unto all, we say these words. Promise not unto your Father that that you do not wish to repay. If a promise is made, fulfill it.

And we say unto Mary these words. We have come to collect your indebtedness. And so it shall be — an eye for an eye, and a tooth for a tooth. Prepare, therefore, for the coming of the Messiah. Do so by word of mouth, by action and deed, for the time of the coming grows close.

The time for the Book of wings is now.

Spread upon your earth glad tidings. Give joy unto your fellow man.

Or we shall give unto you your three thousand years of darkness, and the debt[s] shall be paid in full.

We see thy need, soul [3–3–72–001], and we should answer in this manner. We have given you the sight to see, that of the sight of the mind. We have placed into your keeping the messengers of your people. Yes, we see thy need now, and the healing thy have asked for shall be given and the hand shall be stayed. But do not tarry too long, for the hand that is stayed shall be the messengers'. Give forth that that thy have seen, but do so in an unselfish manner, and your times of trials and tribulations shall end.

Yes, we see thy need, soul [9–1–72–003]....Come before us, and we shall see that that you shall see, and you shall see that that our Father should see.

December 9, 1972: That of God shall be of God's.

Hallowed be the name of the Lord, our Father. Hallowed be the name of His children.

As you should make ready upon this land for the celebration of the one known as Jesus' birth, let each of you place forth upon this night of nights unleavened bread, that that has no yeast. Let each of you take of the wine. Kneel before your God and give thanks that once again your Messiah shall come into you and your world shall give joy everlasting.

Open your hearts. Let the spirit of this one enter, for he left it upon your earth to flow as a river — but not rushing — gently, slowly, ever more beautiful.

Thy have other questions, ask.

"Yes, Aka. I have a question. You speak of a crucifixion taking place on this continent. Was this after Christ was in Israel, and was it an actual crucifixion, or was he put to death in some other manner?"

This was an actual crucifixion, for given in kind, so it was in kind. For as our Father has said, "IT SHALL BE WRITTEN, AND SO IT SHALL BE DONE."

Thy have other questions, ask....

"Aka, [1-21-72-002] asks if you are the same messenger as the one who came to Joseph Smith, who began the Mormon faith?"

We are many. We have come unto many throughout the time of times, for where we dwell there is no time, and where we dwell there is no form. We came upon the earth, this you should call of your home, in the beginning. For that of myself, for I am soul Ray and soul Ray is I, and that his karma should be no more, for that that he was in the beginning, so was I.

Yet, as life was given into his body, we were allowed to enter.

For both of the prophets thy should ask about are one of the same. Yet each shall do that which they were placed upon the earth to do, for they are but instruments of our Father.

And from the beginning and through to the ending is but the same, for life to life, as dust to dust. For does not a wise God place His children upon the earth to hunt and feed that of His kind?

Thy have other questions, ask.

"One moment, Aka." [He turns to his wife, an anthropologist, and asks, *"Could you ask the question?"*]

"Aka, are you also speaking of Nezahualcoyotl?" [Soul Ruth asks.]

Yes, we see thy need. And we speak of the same. And glory be the name of the Lord.

December 15, 1972: Now is the time of the Cherub. For all who are wise to hear, let them hear. For once again, the star of Bethlehem shall burn in your heavens. Give joy and reverence unto all mankind, for the birth of the new Messiah is at hand.

December 22, 1972: And now, upon your day of days, we shall give a full definition of soul Ray's dream.

He dreamed he had many fields to plant upon, and three different types of grain to plant in the many fields.

He dreamed that some of the fields were of rock. And of the fields of rock we shall tell you first, further, for there was a poor farmer who had but a field of rock to plant upon. And he toiled the land year in and year out. And the riches that he sought he never found. And one day, came upon his path a miner, who looked upon the rocky fields and told the farmer to dig within the field and he would find the riches that he sought. And so he did, and there he found gold and silver of many fold.

And of the watery fields he planted upon, there was a fisherman who, day by day, who cast his net into the water, and found not fish at all. And most of the fish he caught were those he dared not keep. And then a miner came to him, and said to him, "Dig beneath the water that you fish upon." And so he did, and there he found the oil to light his many lamps.

And of the fields that were fertile, we tell you this, that no field at all shall yield your riches without your toil. And the heaven you should seek should be that for which you should toil for. And that that you should find upon earth shall be your heaven also.
For your heaven is not in the sky above you, it lies within each separate soul. It dwells upon the earth within the man and woman.

And of the Book you read, and of the many pages you should seek within, to seek the hidden meaning of God's words, when in truth, the truth should dwell in many hearts in many ways. For as there were many paths and many fields to plant upon, these were the many ways to seek your God.

It makes your Father little difference of the name, or the tongue, you should seek Him in. It makes your Father little difference in the manner you should say your prayers. But when you reach your Father, speak as that unto yourselves, and the riches of your reward shall come from within and without.

But the riches that you should seek should lie beneath your feet, for that is where you walk.

Upon this day you should celebrate the coming of the Messiah. Do not plant it in one day, but set your seed upon the earth in many places every day, in every way, and your Father, God, shall see the toil, the loving toil within your hearts. Can you understand of which we speak?

Nay, not fully. But study our words well, for we have not spoke in riddles, as it may seem, but in fullness, with the wisdom our Father should give on us to speak.

Give blessings unto all. And watch the heavens every day, and soon the light that shone before upon the valley of Bethlehem shall shine again, and your new Messiah shall be born unto men.

At this time, we shall give healing upon your earth. For three days, that that you ask for in our Father's name shall be given.

December 29, 1972: Yes, we see thy need, and we should answer in this manner. First, of your question, soul Peter, your question *is* that of the coming of the Messiah.

And we should answer first in this manner. Within your mind is the name of the one known as Jesus, and that of the preparation for the entry of those who have reached the Christ state into this one.

As we have said before, there are many who have reached the Christ state.

And through the combination of these shall be the new Messiah.

You asked that he should come walking from the clouds? And we shall answer your question in this manner. When he should first appear unto the Jewish people, and they shall see him first, he shall be standing upon a cloud. And the Jewish nation in their despair shall kneel before him. This was meant so that that that had been written should be fulfilled. And as we have said before, written upon the clouds, written upon the sky, our Father shall make known of this entry in this way. [See *Acts* 1:6–11, *The Revelation of John*, 7:2–12, chapter 10, 14:1–5, 14:14–16, 15:2–4, 19:1–16, 21:1–7, 22–27, 22:1–7, *Zechariah,* chapters 12–14.]

But he should come unto the body form, for is it not written also that that that does not know of earth cannot know of heaven? And those who do not know of heaven cannot know of earth? For he should come to lead you through your thousand years of peace upon your earth. [See *John* 3:1–21 and *The Revelation,* chapters 19–22.]

The spirit was left that it may flow through all mankind. As we have said before, we have come but for one purpose, and that is for the preparation for the coming of the Messiah. And we say unto you, all of you, open your door that we might enter, and therefore, there can be a place prepared within each of you for his coming. [See *John* 14:1–5, 14:15–26, 15:26–27, 16:7–15, 16:19–24, chapter 17, and *The Revelation,* chapter 12.]

But from a mother's womb, so shall he be born. Look within your book of *Revelation*, and you shall see of the same. But hark unto these words.

Our Father has written only upon the Tablets. Man has written upon your pages and your paper; therefore, many things have been extracted from, taken away from that that inspired the men in the beginning to write of the same, and some has been added to by others.

We have come, not to change the Laws, but to fulfill the prophecies of the same. We have come not to change that that was given within Moses' time. We have come not to change that that was given unto Isaiah. We have come not to change that that was given, and the gift that was given, in the one known as Jesus.

But hark unto these words. We have come for this time. We have come from those who should make their entry.

The Coming of the Son of Man. "And there will be signs in the sun, in the moon, and in the stars; and on the earth distress of nations, with perplexity, the sea and the waves roaring; men's hearts failing them from fear and the expectation of those things which are coming on the earth, for the powers of the heavens will be shaken. Then they will see the Son of Man coming in a cloud with power and great glory. Now when these things begin to happen, look up and lift up your heads, because your redemption draws near." *(Luke 21:25–28)*

We have come from those who did say unto our Father, "Send those who know You best to prepare a way for our coming, that our Father's words should not be misinterpreted." [See *John* 14:15–26, 15:26–27, 16:7–15, and 16:19–24.]....

You have other questions, ask.

"Yes, Aka. When you said that the halftimes are over, do you mean that those who die before the coming of the Messiah will not return during the thousand years of peace?"

Nay. Those who choose entry shall come as they wish to come, but they shall come in complete accord and with knowledge and memory of the same.

The 1973 messages on the Preparation for the Coming

February 9, 1973, Aka spoke to a person: There are many tests that you shall set before yourself, and many we shall set before you, and many Lucifer shall set before you.

But remember, we are here but for one purpose, and that is the coming of the Messiah, to prepare a way.

Your thoughts, as the garden has been weeded, "Why should this be allowed?" And we should say unto you, we should provide that that is needed. But plant the field, and we shall add the yeast and the wine. And the multitudes shall be served in the same manner.

February 23, 1973: And now we should say unto thee once again, we have come, not to change the Laws of Moses; we have come, not to change the laws of the one known as Jesus Christ, for they, within themselves, should all be the Laws of God.

But yet, as many words have been spoken, and as Moses did give forth the Laws for a time and a people, and as Jesus did give forth laws for a time and a people — yet, as many have reached the Christ state — and we should say unto thee, come forth unto this time. For as you should build a building upon an old foundation, the new structure of your modern material the foundation could not withstand its weight, and so it should be true in this time of your people.

If a man is a thief, he should remain a thief should he steal a pencen or much more from a man. Yet, if a man should steal for bread upon his table and he should have naught, then go to this man and say unto him, "Steal not from my table, for my table is God's table. And as you should speak unto your God, speak unto me, and I should give from my table in the same manner my God should give."

But if a man should come, as a thief at night, to kill and maim — and if a man should come and coveth that that belongs to another, whether it should be his ass, or in your time, your automobile, or any other thing — but yet, for what he has stolen can be replaced, even though it should bring great hardship upon you. But if a thief should come and steal your soul away, you cannot punish the thief, but only yourself, for no man can steal your soul without your permission.

Yet, there are some who are lost souls who should use their powers of temptation, much as Lucifer should use temptation. But we say unto you, should this happen unto a man, he should say unto this, "Lucifer, get thee behind me," and it shall be gone. But if his strength is not strong enough, then he should go unto those who know of such, and his brother, they should remove this, for this, in itself, you would call a curse.

Moses brings the Ten Commandments to the people. Jesus added "that you love one another."

And we should say unto you these words. Give praise unto your Father in a righteous manner, and your Father should give praise unto you, His children. But give damnation unto your Father, and your Father should give damnation unto His wayward children.

And therefore, we should say unto you, the Fifth Angel walks upon your earth. There shall be many who should tempt your souls, for now is the time of the great Sword, the sword that cuts two ways, both of man and of the land. For as we have said before, where no water flowed, water shall flow. Rivers shall change their courses. Mountains shall bellow forth. Continents shall change their shapes, and man shall change his in the same manner. But if you are righteous before your Lord, fear not, for your Lord is a righteous God.

Prepare within yourselves, each in your own separate ways, a place for the coming of the Messiah. Give love and kindness unto your brother. Give love and kindness, and love and kindness shall be returned.

Walk, therefore, in a righteous path.

March 2, 1973, Aka spoke to another woman: Of your vision, for we should answer in this manner. We have placed unto your hands mighty tools. Bring forth with these tools that that is needed.

Prepare a way unto the coming of the Messiah, for this before all others is your duty, for these things you have promised unto your God.

March 9, 1973: We should place before thee the bread and the wine. And the Earth that shall be coveth by our Lord shall reach into many hearts, there to show them the direction of the way. But our Father has many mansions, and therefore, there shall be many ways, but all leading to the same chamber. The bread shall be the work we have laid before you. The wine shall be the many souls who shall assist you. Bring them forth into the immortal body of man that your Lord, God, may bring blessings unto His children unto the end of the planes of man.

But your Earth shall not end. It is but a beginning, for we are here but for one purpose, and that is in the preparation for the coming of the Messiah.

We are not great. Our Father is mighty. Yet, He is humble himself before His children. And those who should humble themselves before their God shall drink of the wine of life and from the river of forever.

Let this House stand. [See *The Revelation,* chapters 21–22.]

March 16, 1973: And now, we should tell thee once again, for those who should seek our Father's house, and we should tell thee in this manner.

Go unto a quiet place. And there, open thy heart and mind.

And in the silence of thy mind, thy shall find a quiet pool. And as thy enter, there you shall find the throne of our Father.

But you must enter this place with love. And if you do so, you shall find all the candles lit around you. And there shall burn a glorious light.

Cast all things from thy mind, and let that part of you inter self listen unto your Father.

Go deeply, quietly, for it is not a mansion that you seek but your own soul.

And if the soul should cleanse itself, in the quiet of the mind you shall find the kingdom of our Father.

But do not go from church to church, and seeking every door, for you shall find not what you seek, for it dwells within you evermore.

And we should tell you the parable of the Prince to come.

And he had bare to all riches beyond their wildest imagination. But he did not give just to one; he gave to all. And yet, there were some who wanted more than the others, and they stoned this Prince. And yet, he forgave them.

The Prince that shall come once again, as we have said before, shall be the Messiah. Yet, he awaits you now within the quiet place within you minds.

And we shall tell thee of the small girl who ventured far to the healing wells. And yet, she waited long for all the others to bathe.

But because her faith was great, our Father came unto her.

And He spoke these words unto her. He said, "MY DAUGHTER, WHY DO YOU WAIT FOR ALL THE OTHERS TO GO BEFORE YOU FOR THE HEALING?"

And she looked upon the Father in her mind that spoke to her and said,

"Father, that that shall heal me shall be the faith within myself of you. This cannot be used up by the others."

And God looked down upon His child with love. And from His tender eyes have fell a teardrop on this one. And the faith that the child had held before grew like mountains and winds, and land.

Can you understand of which we speak?

March 23, 1973, Aka spoke to another woman: The gift that we have given is that that you should prepare for the coming of the Messiah. We have laid before you the work that is needed for this time. We have brought before you a prophet, that you may use. Tarry not in daydreams and wishful thinking. Use your time and energy for more useful purposes. There is much work to be done.

April 13, 1973: You have other questions, ask.

"Thank you, Aka. [3–23–73–001], of Tucson, a new member of our group…says that numerologically, 'As my first name is a 63, the same as Christ's, and my last name an 81, the repeated phrase of preparing the way for the Messiah has a special attraction or interest for me. I would like to ask if there is anything specific that can be given that I should be doing, not doing, or changing at this time in the preparation?'"

Yes, we see thy need, and we should answer in this manner. Go forth and bring together a group within your area. Further instructions shall be given at a different time.

Bring faith within thyself, and thy shall find faith within others. Give glory unto your God, and your God shall give glory unto thee.

But we should say unto thee in this manner, we are here but for one purpose, and that is the preparation for the coming of the Messiah. Therefore, make that preparation first within yourself, and we shall give you the tools to prepare the way for others.

April 20, 1973: We say unto thee in this manner, we are here but for one purpose, to prepare the way for the coming of the Messiah.

Start that preparation within your heart and soul,

and the earth shall give forth its mighty bounty, and the heavens shall give forth their mighty bounty — and God shall have a place to rest His head.

April 27, 1973: *"Aka, do you have any words for us on the certification of the teachers?"*

Yes, we should answer in this manner. Let the teachers come unto the prophet.

The light of God shines in the Teacher's candle and within the Teacher.

And let the prophet say unto the teachers, "For the teacher can never be greater than his student. And the student can never be greater than his teacher." Let the prophet say unto them, "Take from thy hands all prejudice, that they shall teach in a righteous manner before their God."

They shall serve under the direction of the prophet. They shall learn from your ministers.

And let the ministers stand and take a vow before the teacher that all of their knowledge shall be given freely unto the teacher, and they shall hide nothing from one another.

But we say unto thee in these words, let minister or teacher hide that that has been given from one another, they shall no longer remain of either. And we say unto you in these words, what the Lord has given, the Lord can taketh away. Beware.

For this day we have laid aside that these teachers should be honored. And the Lord, God, shall look upon them, and He shall honor them. And the Council shall be present, and they shall honor them. For we, as they, are but teachers. And we are not great. We are here but for one purpose, as they should be, for the preparation for the coming of the Messiah.

Let not they bring into this work prejudice of any kind. And glory be the name of the Lord....

We shall speak upon this further before you shall hold your meeting.

May 4, 1973: We come as the peacemakers. Fear not that thy should feel our presence.

Open thy heart that we may enter, and thy days of anguish shall be over, for we shall filleth thy cup, and therefore, a rose shall grow without thorns.

A rose without thorns symbolizes the birth or the coming of the Messiah.

Thy wonder within thy mind to whom we speak. Yet we should say unto you these words. The one we should speak unto should hear our words within their soul and should know of the same.

And we say unto you, lo, lo into the Lord, for these are the righteous days. For the Lord should pave His way with water. And if you should walk the path, you should find the bread along the way, and the multitudes shall be fed.

You have brought forth upon this day that that we have suggested. And tomorrow you shall celebrate your day of grace before the Lord. Do so with glad tidings. As we have said before, we have weeded your garden; therefore, we have planted flowers at your feet. But none of these things that we have done could we do alone, or could we have done them without the permission of the One, the High One, that that you would call of God.

And we shall say unto you, of that of the honoring of the teachers, we see of this and we are pleased. And we say unto the teachers, stand forth and receive that honor that is bestowed upon you. But upon that moment, we shall touch you and make our presence known to all.

Editor's note: The spiritual messengers of God were speaking of the naming of teachers, the first to be at the second Annual Meeting of the Association.

May 11, 1973: Yes, we see thy need. And we should answer in this manner. As your wheat should grow ready for harvest, that that we have planted in the many lands, now stand ready to place it in your storehouses. As we have said before, the spirits of God shall be as a brook, the spirits of man shall be as a river that the brook should flow into, the souls of man shall be as an ocean that shall reach the many lands, and all shall flow together, and therefore, all shall be in accord. Therefore, stand ready within thyselves to receive thy bounty.

Blessed be the name of the Lord, for we are not great; we are but the servants of our Father, God, and we are here but for one purpose. That in itself is the preparation for the coming of the Messiah, and as has been told before, to bring forth upon your earth your thousand years of peace, but not as you count, but as our Father counts.

May 22, 1973: And we should say unto you, your seed is now ready for harvest, and the many fields shall come forth upon the land. Prepare yourselves within, that you can prepare for the one purpose of our coming. For we are not great; we are here but for one purpose, to prepare a way for the coming of a Messiah.

Now is the time of the Cherub. And the Fifth Angel walks upon your earth.

June 1, 1973: As a fountain should push forth as knowledge the waters of the earth, as the tree should reach upward unto the heavens, so should your truth be. For thy shall not give false witness unto any man, for truth shall be thy saber in the days ahead. For as a river should flow, and yet, as you stand in one place you shall never see the same river twice, for new water shall flow past you every moment, and so it should be with knowledge. But truth should come in many forms. And because one should speak differently, yet meaning the same, thy should not walk away from knowledge that is truth.

Should a man come before thee, and yet, within thy mind, say, "Look upon the earth, for it is not there," do not call this man a liar, but store his knowledge for another day, and let the time pass, and through time the truth shall be known unto thee. And so it should be true with prophets upon the earth this day. Choose your words wisely, yet come forth in truth.

But yet, and we say unto you, your God is the God of the living, not of the dead. And we have come forth but for one purpose, and that is the preparation for the coming of the Messiah.

June 8, 1973: And first, we should say into these words. Give that unto your Lord that is praise. Give that unto your Lord that is your sorrow. Give that unto your Lord that is happiness. Open your doorway and let the Lord share all things, and thy shall never walk alone, for in your hour of desperation you shall reach within that quiet place that the [internal, eternal] candle shall burn, and therefore, find the Lord within. Yet, we see that within each soul's daily tasks is all part of God, our Father.

Yet we should say once again, if thy should give a gift unto thy brother, give it in such a manner that you should expect nothing in return. Only then can thy give the true blessings that are within man to give to one another.

And now we should answer this question you have had within your minds of the shroud.

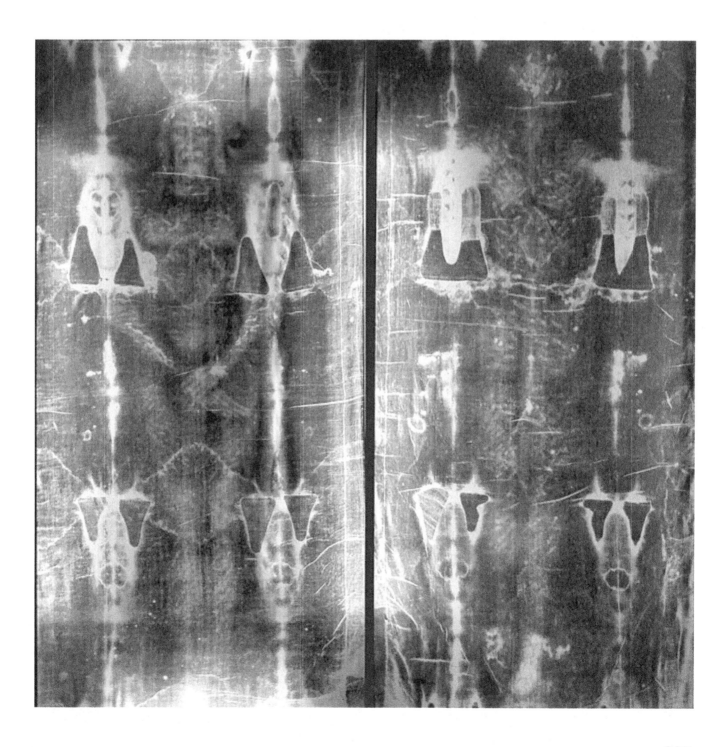

First, we should answer in this manner, as the body of the one known as Jesus was taken, therefore, from the cross, that those who bare him and the bearers who carried him brought for the body, and there, both of the first wrappings were taken place, but the ointments were first applied to the body. This was done very soon after the death itself, as the oils and the ointments of the chemicals within the same were used to cleanse the body, and then the body was wrapped much, as you would know, in a mummified state. After this was done, cloth that was soaked in the same ointment was used in such a manner as you would cover a body with a blanket.

Now, as we have said before, as those who would come upon the morn, therefore they found within the tomb both shrouds, as you would know it. The true shroud would be that into which the body was wrapped of cloth. Yet, the second was also true, and this is which you have spoke about.

The wrappings themselves were never recovered from the tomb.

They were passed from living disciple to living disciple, yet there to stay with John in exile.

But the impression, or the picture form, which should show upon this shroud was a distorted, at best. Yet, if you should mix the same chemicals, secreting that which come from the body as the soul should leave the body and make ready for the resurrection, you shall find that it should give you picture form, much of the manner unto which you have.

But you must understand, from boyhood to manhood, this one known as Jesus was touched by God, and therefore, as the scars of life should show upon each man and woman, so should the scars of goodliness, that which should become the blessed one, the Lamb of God.

We shall answer into your words once again. Make your questions in a direct form. You must realize, for us to use unto this one known as soul Ray, and then the passing of the information that is needed, and the sources unto which your questions are gathered from are many, therefore we have looked into the question of this one. We saw those unto which he had mentioned. Yet we are not great. We bring forth the knowledge that is placed before us.

> *We are here but for one purpose; that is the preparation for the coming of the Messiah. Therefore we say unto you all, bear not false witness unto any man.*

Take of each other's knowledge and share it equally, as we have shared knowledge with you.

Make you questions in a direct manner, for our time is short, for the use of Ray's body, and overuse could burn it, as you would know; the internal organs, of both body, mind, overuse could destroy it....

We have sent teachers. Yet we come now to prepare the way. Prepare that way within yourself, and give it unto others in the same manner that the Master would give it unto us, and you — with love, compassion.

> *Learn that it is not the knowledge that should come from written words, but words that are put into written writing that are wisdom.*

As a teacher should teach always in a simple manner, our God said not words unto His children they could not understand. Say not words unto the children you shall serve.

June 19, 1973: Yes, we see thy need, and we shall tell you

the parable of the Seven Spirits of God.

And God had sent them forth to plant their fields, for He should make them ready to create your earth. And in the beginning, each helped the other in the toil of the planting of the fields. But as the time of harvest grew near, they began to argue. They began to argue, and to separate. And they continued to argue. And the fields ripened in the fields, yet they argued even more. And the grain they had planted rotted in the field. And then the Lord called them back before Him. And each stood to blame the other that they had not brought back unto their Lord their harvest.

And the Lord sent them forth again to plant the field. And again, they argued and the fields did not become planted. And this time they were afraid to go back unto their Lord. But the Lord, God, appeared before them and said unto them, "THY SHALL PLANT YOUR FIELDS OVER AND OVER AGAIN UNTIL YOU COME BACK UNTO ME WITH THE LESSON YOU HAVE LEARNED FROM THE PLANTING OF THE FIELDS."

Time passed. Days passed. Years passed. Thousands of years passed.

And then one day the seven walked before their Lord, and with them they bore the grain they had harvested from the many fields.

And the Lord looked unto them and said, "WHAT HAVE YOU LEARNED?"

And they spoke forth together and said into these words, "Oh, Lord, we have learned this lesson, that to plant a field and to harvest a field each of us must depend upon the other; none of us can be greater than the other, that each of us must use the other's talent."

And so the Lord sent them forth to create the Earth. And each depended upon the other, for one who laid upon the earth the ferment of many kinds, and the other who brought forth the animal life of many kinds, and the other who created the ocean and water and streams, and the other who planted life within the streams, and the other who brought forth man, and the other who brought forth woman, and the last who breathed life into all and did place upon ferment on your earth.

And they went before their God. And God looked upon the Earth and said unto them, "IT IS GOOD, FOR IT OF OUR KIND, OF OUR LIKENESS."

Now we say unto you these words. You have sought to blame many things upon your shortcomings, when the fault had laid within yourselves. You have cast blame, one upon the other, and we have watched and God has watched.

And we say unto you once again, we are not here to make you great in the eyes of men. We are not here to make ourselves great in the eyes of men.

We are here for but for one purpose, and that is the preparation for the coming of the Messiah. For this in itself to happen, there must be unity within your groups.

We have laid before you a prophet, that he may use his knowledge to guide unto you. Yet he is overtaxing his body. This in itself would not cause a problem, because of the overtaxing the body which he would tire and stop. But we have spared him but for this one purpose. If you cannot again find unity and purpose within yourselves, as the Lord has given, the Lord shall taketh away. He is of many times. Yet we should send him forward once again.

But you within yourselves shall continue planting the field until you come before your Lord in such a manner that you know how to depend on one another. This in itself must be your philosophy.

The one medicine that he must have is tranquility in his daily life. He sees many things, yet he is but like yourselves, yet of human form, of blood and bone, of body, of soul, of spirit, and of mortal body.

We say unto you that this way must be prepared....

"Was the destruction of the island of Atlantis remaining in the time of Noah because of the earth's slipping on its axis or because of an atomic explosion?"

First were the atomic explosions; second was the earth's slipping upon its axis. Both were interrelated to parts of the same. That of the splitting of the atom, as you know it, is but a minor thing from the power unto which they had harnessed, for they had harnessed that of the cosmic power, the splitting of the cosmic rays within themselves, therefore, the changing within your atmosphere of the amount of cosmic energy laid forth upon the earth and into each individual. This is why your form did change. And so it shall again.

But fear not, for those who do not wear the mark of the Beast shall walk upon this new heaven and new earth, and live within the thousand years of peace, and shall see the Messiah walk upon your earth.

July 2, 1973: And we should say unto thee, as we have said before, as the water should be as the spirit of man. Yet we should tell unto thee of the parable of the river that came from nowhere, the river that had no beginning and no ending, and so it should be with the spirits of man, and so it should be with the spirits of God.

Take forth your ark, the ark of the soul, and let it flow into the river, that the river should flow unto the many lands. And we say unto thee, look unto the east, yet look among you, for we are here but for one purpose, that is in the preparation for the coming of the Messiah.

Make this way within your hearts.

Open the door that we may enter.

July 6, 1973: And we should say unto thee these words.

As we have said before, thy have found the rock unto which the brook should flow — and that that should flow from the brook shall be the spirits of God — and the spirits shall flow into the river, and the river shall be the spirits of man — and the river shall flow unto your oceans.

And as each pebble is separate and apart, so should be the souls of men be separate and apart, but yet, again it shall flow unto the many nations. It shall flow unto all tongues. It shall flow unto all mankind, for we are here but for one purpose, that in itself is the preparation for the coming of the Messiah.

And we say unto thee, as thy should plant a field...and go on to plant another, go back and weed each field. Do not become so busy that thy cannot weed the fields and cannot pick the grain that comes from that. Always remember from which you have come. If you may do this, you shall know where you are going.

We have placed unto your hands this man whom you call the prophet, yet he is not great and we are not great, for we are all but humble servants before our Lord. Go unto the valley and pick the lilies. Share them with one another. Go unto the valley and pick the fruit and the berries that should grow wild there. But should the birds come, do not drive them away, for they must eat also. For what our Lord has provided, all may share.

For did it not be said that the darkness shall be lifted, that the light should come through, and that knowledge should be shared by all of mankind. If you may do this, then your thousand years of peace are but of hand.

Give forth the love of our Father unto one-tenth unto your fellow man.

But if you should go unto a desert, and therefore, find a well, and it is sweet and good unto taste, and yet, you should leave of this well, take some of the water with you and the memory of the water shall remain forever within your minds, your soul, your body, and the immortal body of the same.

Glory be the name of the Lord.

July 9, 1973: And we shall say once again unto these words. As in the time of Moses, there were some who should wait their forty years, therefore, for a time of learning. There were some who were hasty and should cross the river before the Lord should give unto them their time. And for those who did so, there was no return. Yet, for those who waited and had faith in the Lord, all came in complete.

The light that shown above came forth unto the one known as Jesus.

It was the same light that had come forth to guide Moses and his people, yet it was more brilliant and more beautiful than all light that had been seen before. But yet, each was for a separate time.

And we should say unto thee into these words. We have come not for the time of Moses. We have come not for the time of Jesus. But we have come now in this manner to prepare a way, and this way should be the preparation for the coming of the Messiah.

Yet, we have come with the knowledge of your day, this day, upon your earth, and of your tomorrows, that new wisdom may be placed upon the earth, new understanding, that brethren should not kill brethren, that love shall come upon the earth,

and so it shall be in fulfillment....

Thy have other questions, ask.

"Aka, regarding his future, he says, 'Do you have any suggestions as to how I could be of better service to humanity?'"

We shall say unto thee unto this manner. We have come not to make man great. We have come but for one purpose and that is the preparation for the coming of the Messiah.

Therefore, we place before you the bread and the wine.

Apply the yeast, and the multitudes shall eat from the same, and therefore, you yourself shall have a hand in feeding all.

There is much knowledge that we have placed before you. But yet again, true wisdom must come from within — that that you see, that that you hear, and the opening of the mind to understand. Take into thy mind, much as you would take into your stomach, that which you can digest at one time. If you should eat smaller quantities, your stomach should digest it. Do the same with the mind, as the digestion has completed then take that on within the mind that should bring forth more knowledge. Soon you will find the mind has expanded and grown and is capable of taking great quantities of knowledge at one time.

Thy have other questions, ask.

"Aka, he asks, 'I have been told by several psychics that I would be doing another type of work some day. Do you have any comment on that?'"

We have just answered that question.

July 27, 1973: Now we say unto thee in this manner, in these words. We have placed some of you in positions that are that of labor. Your knowledge is great. We have placed some of you in positions to do certain jobs. But we say unto you, in the eyes of God all is mighty.

Look through the eyes of God unto yourselves, and you shall see that each within themselves are very important.

But you can build once again both an ark and a dike, that your 300 years of darkness shall not come upon the earth — and the 300 shall go unto 3,000 — that man should not walk backward and be that much less than the smallest animal upon the earth, that the way shall be prepared for his [the Messiah's] coming.

Prepare, therefore, within each of you that way. But prepare it in such a manner that you should look unto yourselves, and see the righteousness of your paths.

July 30, 1973: But we should say unto you unto these words, that as man should ride upon the river, and he should run the same river over and over down in his boat through the rapids, past the falls, into the clear water, and yet into the sea itself — and if he should do so day by day, then one day he becomes careless and he forgets from where he came, and where he has been, and that that he has to do. And so his craft crashes against the rapids, and his body is thrown over the waterfalls, and piece by piece his many parts should flow into the ocean. But just in the same moment he could have been careless and lost his soul, and his spirit, and his immortal body.

For there shall be many who shall say unto you, do of this and do of that; there shall be mothers and daughters, there shall be those who should hold you to the earth and bind you in such a manner that your soul can no longer fly free and give birth unto that unto which the Lord has placed within your hands.

There is beauty in sorrow, as you have seen. And there is sorrow in beauty, as you have seen. But all parts are part of God, and all parts are part of man down his wandering, watery path to the sea. And if he should reach the continents of the land, he should take all of these with him and the memory of all.

But we say unto you, you are of all parts of what you have been before. This has brought you forth to this time, to this place. Give praise unto your Lord.

But we shall say unto you into these words.

> *We cannot interfere with you free choice. God has given this in the beginning, and God shall not take it away.*

But we are here but for one purpose. That purpose within itself is for the preparation for the coming of the Messiah. Each reading that we have used soul Ray's body has been for that purpose. We chose of this body because deep within it lay the wisdom, and the memory of where it had been, within the soul and spirit form and the immortal body. But yet, we knew it had much to learn, much to remember. We placed within his hands and his mind that to teach, and that to heal, and that to teach unto others.

We lay before you your free choice. You have seen unto where you have been.

You may go unto many others, and many others will tell you other tales. But we say unto you, a prophet shall be known by his deeds, not by how loud or coarse he can talk, or by how much profanity he can throw upon others, for a true prophet should only have time for that that lies before him.

August 3, 1973, at the end of a health reading, Aka said: We shall say unto thee into these words. You have yet within your science to find the key that lies within the mind that should bring forth and stop your aging process. Within the mind lies the key to reverse the process, and therefore, taking mind and body slowly back into the youthful condition it once was.

But we should say unto thee into these words.

As an old oak stands and looks upon the young, would it trade its knowledge for their youth?

Thy have thy faith within God, and God has His faith within you.

This within itself is the most important of all things, for the doors that shall open shall be beautiful –

A rose without thorns spiritually symbolizes the birth or coming of the Messiah.

for roses shall be placed without thorns.

August 7, 1973: But you are building within a world that is foreign to the thought of many things. It is not by the use of deceit that we have advised you, but by the use of the building and the preparing of the way for the coming of the Messiah, which is our main purpose above all.

Soon we shall name others. Their acceptance shall be witnessed by no one other than those who should come forth and be counted. Can you understand of which we speak?

"Yes."

To be ordained before God.

August 20, 1973: We say unto you unto these words,

we have come but for one purpose, that purpose is the preparation for the coming of the Messiah. We are not great.

August 27, 1973, Aka spoke to a person: We shall say unto thee unto these words. We have come forth but for one purpose. That, in itself, as we have told you before you were born, to prepare a way for the coming of a messiah.

The Eagle is here. A way has been provided for the fulfillment of your life. That which you have asked for has been given.

The Lord, God, has placed into your hands free choice.

September 5, 1973, Aka spoke at end of an individual's life reading: Take forth this knowledge unto which we have given you. Seek out honesty by being honest with yourselves and others. Seek out love by giving love. And your cup shall runneth over.

We say unto you, the time is near at hand when the things we have mentioned within the readings, the time of the famine, shall be upon the earth. Take forth from the knowledge and prepare within yourself for this time. But do more.

Prepare for the day that you shall meet your self, that of your real self within you, and in that preparation you shall prepare yourself for the coming of the Messiah.

The Fifth Angel walks upon your earth. Earthquakes, tornadoes, hurricanes, fire shall blight the earth.

Now is the time of the Cherub.

September 7, 1973: Yes, we see thy need. And we should say, as we have said before, that if thy should go into the desert to search for a well for water, and you came upon a new well that should flow of new water, and the water was sweet and good, would you drink from it, or would you ask its age?

Yet, as you journeyed farther and you found an old well, that the water had flowed long before man had entered upon this ground, would you say unto the well, "I cannot drink of your water because you are old?"

And we say unto thee unto these words, that nothing upon your earth remains the same, only a thought form that is trapped, a thought form when the door is closed and no more can enter. So take of the old and the new, and that that is yet to come, and bring it forth into knowledge. Let it be born upon the earth. Prepare, therefore, a way within yourselves.

And we should say once again, for those who would listen, for the yoke of love that you should carry, there shall be much work for all, and there shall be hands to perform this work.

But it must be done together, much as the old and new well both play this, their parts, within the world's system of man.

And so it must be in heaven as in earth. For as we have told you the parable of the Seven Spirits, all must work together in unisance. Take, therefore, not unto yourself to say, "This is my path and I can only go one way. I will accept only this help or that help." But accept the hand that is handed to you in a friendly manner.

End your prejudice unto one another. And the promises our Father has brought forth shall come forth as roses in the desert. Mountains shall grow, and the kingdom of God shall be born forth into man's hearts and souls, and spirits and immortal bodies.

There shall be storms. There shall be those who should try to interfere with this work. But it shall not happen.

Bring forth unto the multitudes the words we have given unto you.

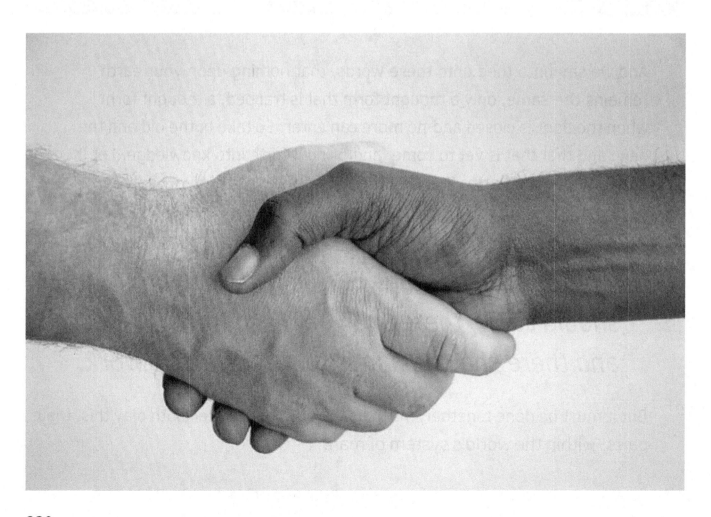

Bring forth unto the knowledge, for it is not our knowledge, but a knowledge that was flown as free as a breeze that came from our Father.

The knowledge was for all who should seek.

We shall say unto you once again these words.

We are here but for one purpose, and that purpose shall be in the preparation for the coming of the Messiah. We have chosen the tools at hand. We have [both] brought forth fruit unto your gardens, and the fruit shall bear seed that more fruit shall grow again, and again. We shall see to your needs. Glory be the name of the Lord.

September 11, 1973: And now we should tell unto the parable.

For as the Seven Spirits so, upon the Lord's instructions, did create the earth and all within it, the Third Spirit looked upon the small ponds and meadows, and within it he delicately placed that which you would call the water lily.

The other spirits stood beside him, and said unto him, "Why should you place such a thing in this place? It cannot last."

And the Seventh [Third] Spirit said unto this one, "For it shall be a reminder unto mankind."

And the Seventh Spirit said, "How should this be so? How could it be a reminder unto mankind?"

And the Third Spirit said that, "Man in his evolution through time is always in such a hurry to reach where he is going that he soon forgets where he has been. But the water lily grows from the bottom of the pond, and floats to the surface, and therefore, to place a beautiful blossom for man to see. And so it shall be unto man, that he may see that though man should travel through the darkness of time, his reward should be that of surfacing and giving beauty unto mankind and unto himself and unto God."

All of these thought for a while.

And the First Spirit said unto them, "Come, I shall show you what the Third should show you upon the earth. But we must go forward in time.

"First we shall stop here where man is created.

"And you see the entries taking place, one by one, and two by two, and three by three.

And now look forward.

And now you see this one who should come forth that should be called of the Prophet. And he should come upon the earth, and therefore, be called by our Father unto His first born, for he came as Adam, and he came forth as the one known as Jesus Christ.

But look between the times."

And the Fourth Spirit said, "Yes, we can see of this. But come and let me show you what I can see."

And so they went forward in time yet again a short period, and looked upon the earth of that called the Americans. And there, once again stood the Prophet. They were not amazed, for they knew of their Father's wishes.

But the Prophet stood before the dawn upon a small hill. And beside him stood a great chief, not only in wisdom, but in size. Yet the Prophet was small compared to this great chief. But as the dawn cameth forward, a shroud of light from our Father surrounded this one of the Prophet. And the great chief knelt before this one to grasp his garment. Yet the Prophet gently raised him up to his full height, and he said unto the chief, "It shall not be the size of man that should make the man, but it should be the size of his wisdom and that unto which he shall use it."

And the Fifth Spirit stood forth and said, "Then let's go forward in time still yet again, and I shall show you what I see that the Third Spirit's meaning is."

And they looked upon the earth. And they looked upon the heavens. And from the heavens they heard unto these words spoken, "FOR THE HALFTIMES SHALL COME TO AN END AND BE NO MORE."

And out upon the vast lands death came forward upon the earth. And one by one, and two by two, and three by three, those who had evolved and evolved again without meaning ceased to be, and there were no more of these, for they were cast unto the bottomless pit. And the lost souls were cast unto the bottomless pit. And all became an eternal fire within the same.

And the Second Spirit looked upon the earth, and said, "Then I shall show you what I see that the Third Spirit had meant."

And a breeze blew forth upon the earth, and the fires were quieted, and from the earth sprung new life. Some of these souls were very old who should enter; some were very young who should enter. But all that entered came with a common cause, to reach and build their thousand years upon the earth. And they looked upon the earth, and among them stood the one we shall say unto thee is the Messiah yet to come. And from heavens and the universes came those of their kind, for they in truth had also learned from the earth's karma that they must be shepherds also, for they are brothers, all in one, and sisters, all in one, all before mankind.

And so we have told unto thee the parable of the halftimes and their ending.

You have questions, ask.

"Yes, Aka. [5-4-73-002]...and she would like a life reading."

Yes, we have before us the body, the soul, and the spirit, and the immortal body within the same, and therefore, we have before us the records.

Therefore, we find this one — yes — born in the year of the deer. This one came forth in original form upon the planet [Plutarius, Butarius]. Yet, much as the entry upon the other planets, and the souls did enter, this one was fearful of the entry. And she long looked upon the stars. And one glittered within her mind more than all the others.

And she said unto them around her, "For that shall be my home. That is my land, not this."

And those of the wise said, "But you have been selected for this planet. You have free choice, and in this choice you have been, chosen this planet for entry."

She said unto them, "Then who should I see, who should I talk to that I may take my choice elsewhere into the land unto which my soul says is home?"

And the wise one said unto her, "Take it into the Lord."

And so she dwelt through long journey, across the rocky paths unto the mighty mountains, and through the lava beds, and through the meadows and the fields. She had become hungry, for now, these things that man called food were important to her.

Yet she lay in despair and said, "Oh, Lord, oh, Lord, where art Thy?"

And the Lord spoke back unto her, and He said, "I AM HERE, WITHIN THEE."

And she said unto this One, "Then why should I have journeyed so far to have found You?"

And the Lord said unto her, "FOR IT WAS NOT ME THAT YOU WERE SEEKING, BUT YOURSELF. YOU HAVE CHOSEN FIRST THIS PLANET, AND NOW YOU WISH ANOTHER. THEREFORE, THIS GIFT SHALL BE GRANTED UNTO THEE. BUT YOU SHALL FIND YOUR OWN WAY UNTO THIS PLACE CALLED EARTH."

And the words were familiar unto her. And she said unto the Lord, "But where should I go?"

And He said, "GO BACK UNTO WHICH YOU HAVE COME, FOR YOU SHALL BE YOUR OWN JUDGE."

And the Lord placed before her food and drink, and it strengthened her body, and she went back unto the village unto which she was born.

And day by day, within her was a waiting time of a promise yet to be fulfilled. And yet, she married, and bore children, and loved the land unto which she dwelt. And as she became old, her time of departure did come, and she passed beyond the other side.

And she met there many who were of her kind, but they spoke of different things. And she said unto them, "Where have you come from?"

And they said unto her, "We are those of the earth."

And then she knew her promise had been fulfilled. But yet she looked back upon her planet and her loved ones.

She lingered long between the planes, not knowing of which direction to take. Yet, upon the earth she watched as man evolved. And she saw the blessed one born upon her own planet, and she saw the blessed one born on the plant of earth.

And she went into the masters and she said, "But earth is much as my own planet was. Why do I linger for it so?"

And the masters said unto her, "Go forth and seek out that which you need to satisfy thy soul."

And so she found entry upon this thy call the American continent. And she stood upon the shoreline as the one who walked upon the water did come forth.

And she rushed forward to grasp his hands, and he gently laid them forward, and there, in each hand, were those strange marks.

And she said unto him, "But yet, I have seen you die upon that faraway land." And she said unto him, "Why have you come here?"

And he looked at her, and to say these words, "For I am here to take care of my Father's business, as a good son should."

And she said unto him, "May I travel with you?"

And he said unto her, "Yes, you may travel, but only until the Eagle flies. And then you must make your own decisions upon this earth."

And so she traveled far, and attained great knowledge.

But in the day that the Eagle flew, she looked upon this one they called the Morning Star, the Master, and said, "Master, now I shall follow the Eagle, for it has been my choice."

And he said, "Then go unto the Eagle. But the next time you see his flight in full you shall know of the announcement of our coming, for there will be those who were sent to prepare the way."

And now, you have evolved upon this time.

And we say unto you, as we have come with a mighty comet upon your earth, we have brought forth gifts and greetings.

For once again a comet shall fly through your air, through the earth's atmosphere.

First, there was a comet of our arrival.

Comet Bennett passed closest over Earth on March 25, 1970. With it the spiritual messengers of God say they arrived. It's brilliant light shone in the heavens for one-third of the Earth to see at a time. And is shone brightly through April and May 1970, while Aka spoke to us. This photo was taken on April 3, 1970, the first day we recorded Aka's words.

Now this comet shall claim the changing of a time. And the earth shall now begin its mighty change to clothe itself in other forms.

Yet we say unto you, for the wise to hear, let them hear; for the wise to see, let them, yea [see].

For upon the heavens look forth. Count 11 days from the first sighting of the comet, and we shall once again be seen within your heavens, to give proof unto mankind of our presence.

The newly discovered comet on March 18, 1973, Kohoutek, became visible to the eye in late November 1973. The comet reached perihelion on 28 December 1973. The comet brightened to an apparent magnitude of 2.8 by 22 December 1973 before becoming indiscernible to ground-based observers due to Kohoutek's conjunction with the Sun; between 24 and 31 December the comet was within 10° of the Sun. During this period, the comet experienced a surge in brightness that — although not clearly observable from the Earth's surface — placed it in the echelon of great comets. Kohoutek was at its brightest during this period, becoming a roughly –3rd magnitude object. Though the comet was then its brightest, it could only be observed by scientific instrumentation and astronauts on Skylab. For most ground observers, Kohoutek only reached as bright as magnitude 0 when it emerged from the Sun's glare in January 1974. It quickly faded beyond naked-eye visibility later that month and was last observed in November 1974. Kohoutek was predicted to be the comet of the century, but was less bright than expected. The brightest comet was most likely the newly discovered comet Bennett with which Aka arrived upon Earth in late March-early April 1970.

Aka continued the life reading: Your life, you have brought forth both of the greed, the need to serve unto yourself more than unto others.

This, by leaving your home planet, you did not think of the need of your people, but only of your own need.

And even as you followed the Master upon the earth, you thought only, therefore, within yourself.

Did the Sons of God come to Earth from Mars, which some call the "planet of war"?

And once, again as the Eagle should take flight, these thoughts are still there. Cast them aside. Prepare in thyself a place for others, and in doing so, many shall prepare within themselves a place for you.

For the Lord has not placed us upon the earth for idle curiosity. We are here but for one purpose, and that is, within itself, the preparation for the coming of the Messiah.

September 21, 1973: And now we should say unto thee these words. Blessed be the meek upon the earth. Yet, blessed be the strong. Blessed be those among you who should build the temple of God within you.

But we say unto thee, we have come not to change the Laws of Moses. We have come not to change the testimony of the one known as Jesus Christ. We have come but for one purpose, that in itself is the preparation for the coming of the Messiah. Glory be the name of the Lord.

Moses with the Ten Commandments

But we should say unto thee, each of you, for in stone upon the mountain was cast in flame and brought forth unto mankind. And the tablets you brought from planet to planet, and the knowledge therein, that unto which you call your Ten Commandments, they are the words of God. Yet, He asks unto you but two things — love unto Him one tenth of the love that He should return unto you; do so in the same manner unto your fellow man.

Coveth not that that should belong to another. That thy should overcome thy karma, understand into which that that each of you are. Only by understanding can you cast the seed upon the earth that should grow the fields that should prepare the way for the coming.

September 28, 1973: And we should say unto thee unto these words.

As the river flows unto the ocean, it should change of the ocean; as the ice should melt from the mountains, so the rivers should change. Therefore, your earth is changing.

Fear not.

Now is the time of the Cherub. The Fifth Angel walks upon your earth. Glory be the name of the Lord.

We are here but for one purpose, that in itself is the preparation for the coming of the Messiah.

October 2, 1973: Yes, we see thy need, and we should answer in this manner. Give that unto yourself that belongs unto yourself. Give that unto your fellow man that belongs unto your fellow man. Give that unto God that belongs to God. But as the sun should come forth upon your earth, and for the rays of the sun, so shall be the souls of man.

Thy have thought in thy mind, "How should I climb the ladder unto my Lord?" And we should answer in this manner, our Father has many mansions. But think of man and the souls of man as the rays of the sun that should filter forth upon your earth unto all proportions. Think of night, and think of day. Yet the sun shall shine where darkness lies, and darkness shall lie where the sun should shine. For think of that hidden place within your mind. Go unto that hidden place and find the knowledge therein, for we have placed upon the Earth teachers for all the mansions.

We have come not to change the laws of Moses. We have come not to change the laws and gifts of the one known as Jesus Christ.

We have come but for one purpose, that purpose is the preparation for the coming of the Messiah upon your Earth.

And so it shall be.

Glory be the name of the Lord....

Aka said, after another's life reading: And we shall say unto you these words of wisdom. We have brought forth the wine and the bread. Provide, therefore, the yeast. But be a student, and then a teacher. We have placed thou upon the Earth.

But look forth upon the one who still washes the feet of his disciples, and you shall find the way, for we are here but for one purpose, that purpose is in the preparation for the coming of the Messiah.

Take forth the wisdom and the knowledge we have given unto you, and life shall bear life, and kind shall bear kind, for thy halftimes have ended.

Then, October 5, 1973, Aka spoke to another after her life reading: At times, you now on this earth plane of this time, you, more than all others, should know that the mark of the Beast that can be placed upon man; therefore, do not use the abilities given unto you in folly, or once again the mark of Cain, the mark of the Beast, shall be placed upon you. Bring forth this that you have seen, for we are here but for one purpose, that purpose is the preparation for the coming of the Messiah. Your abilities of the mind have been restored, but remember unto these words, that that the Lord has given, the Lord can taketh away. For the half-times are over.

We have placed the bread and the wine at your feet.

Within the Teacher's candle, and within the Teacher, shines the light of God

We have shown you where you have been, that you should know where you are going. Cast aside these follies....

Bring forth your gifts and your abilities. Bring forth the wine the Lord has given unto you to give.

> *Open the door and we shall enter, and the cup shall runneth over....*

The healing that you have asked for shall be given.

Then, October 9, 1973, Aka said to another after the life reading: You shall listen unto these words we have spoken unto you. They shall confuse you. But come forth, and we shall provide the bread and the yeast, for we say unto you, we are here but for one purpose, that is in the preparation for the coming of the Messiah.

> *Our Father has many mansions.* Our Father should ask unto you, as you ask unto Him, "PREPARE THEREFORE A PLACE THAT I MAY LIE MY HEAD AND REST MY SOUL."

We have shown of you the two sides of the Sword. And as you were told before of a future yet to come, now you have been told again of a future yet to come, the fulfillment of the same. But as you were given free choice of entity, free choice to come forth, open the door that we may enter,

> *for in God's house there are many hands that are needed for the preparation of his coming.*

Glory be the name of the Lord.

October 23, 1973, following another's life reading, Aka said: Now we should say unto you, we have shown you of your past. Now we shall show unto you that that should lay before you.

But first, we should say unto you these words. The Eagle is in flight.

We are here but for one purpose, that is in the preparation for the coming of the Messiah, that peace may come unto your Earth in your lifetime.

But yet this is your choice.

The grass is green and beautiful all about you. The hills, the mountains, and the springs. Love lays but at your fingertips. We have brought you into a land of milk and honey where all of your wants and even your needs are taken in abundance, yet you see them not. We have brought you here that we may speak to you. We have spoken to you long ago in your before time, for we are those that were known as Re or Arcan, for we are Aka. Your search for our knowledge is but at your fingertips.

All you must do is ask.

October 27, 1973: *Yes, Aka, [10-27-73-002] who is here tonight asks...'What significance on our own personal lives will the comet have, and will it affect each one differently? Also, how can this be related to the influences of the other planets?'"*

We shall answer the question, for it shall be general information.... Therefore, we should answer in this manner.

The comet shall affect your Earth. For the ignorant, they shall think of it as the last sign of the Earth. For those who profess great knowledge shall think of it as just another passing within the heavens. But unto each of you, the passing shall come forth in this manner — for as we have said before, we are here but for one purpose, that is in the preparation for the coming of the Messiah; therefore the sign that we have promised shall be seen by the whole Earth, to observe the might of our Father. It shall be the brightest star in the heavens.

Count, therefore, 11 days from the first day it can be seen with the naked eye, and there in the heavens above you shall be a sign for each of you — for as it has been said once before, "He did cometh with the morning star, and he did go back unto the same." Therefore, in the hours before your dawn, it shall be the brightest.

In November 1973, Kohoutek became bright enough to be visible to the naked eye. The ion component of the comet's tail was first noted on November 21 accompanying the brighter dust component. Then Kohoutek gave an unexpected wave of it's long tail 11 days later as it approached the Sun, as Aka had said.

But all of your earth shall know of our coming and that unto which we have come to do upon your earth.

But you ask of the effect upon the other planetary systems within the same, upon the galaxies and galaxies. Similar signs have been cast forth upon God's domain, that all may see and know of the same.

You yourselves have seen unto each of you that which you would call of your UFOs. These have been sent forth from other planetary systems to observe the effect upon the Earth. Yet, they should look unto the effect upon themselves, for our Father has sent forth these words, "THE HALFTIMES ARE OVER. PREPARE THERE, EACH WITHIN YOURSELVES."

But the promise that our Father left upon the Earth for a thousand years of peace, if man heeds our words, you shall have of such; your year shall be the year of 1999. But count not as you would count, but count each day as a thousand years. [Remember, Jesus said, "But of that day and hour no one knows, not even the angels in heaven, nor the Son, but only the Father." (*Mark* 13:32)]

If the messages that we have brought forth upon the Earth is not heeded, the other planetary systems shall go on without you, and the Earth shall go unto 3,000 years of darkness, and you shall dwell as you once did in caves before the coming of the Sons of God.

You have other questions, ask.

"Yes, Aka, there was an additional part to this question. 'Do the comets carry souls between spheres? And what is the difference between the makeup of the comet compared to the makeup of the sun?'"

We shall answer in this manner. As the cosmic dust should gather forth unto the same unto the heavens, and therefore, given heavenly guidance, your comet, as you would speak of it, is brought forth first in the form much as a new world would be. But then it is cast from any orbit and sent forth in its direction.

The sun, as you would know of it, is not a planet, but a star. Some would say that this is a dying star. Look beyond, and you shall find that it is yet a living star, one who a planet shall be born from. Our words are contrary to your astronomical thoughts. Yet there are many truths.

You have other questions, ask.

"Thank you, Aka. [10-27-73-002] who is here tonight asks, 'What is meant in the Bible, there will be people seen coming from the heavens and people from the earth; the earth shall run red with blood?' She asks, 'Is this an actual battle or a war for men's minds?'"

We have placed, therefore, unto soul Ray's mind the vision. We placed, therefore, the vision that as the fuse was lit and came from Europe and went into the land of Israel — and from the fuse entered many lands and many unto battle — and therefore, your world began to smolder — and all of those of the Jewish belief, therefore, should see before them coming from the heavens the first signs of the one you would know as Jesus Christ, yet he should come forth in a form that they would know, and they shall bow before him. Yet, your world should runneth red with blood, for there shall be in reality, in the valley of Armageddon [Megiddo], so shall the valley [battle] be fought on Heaven and Earth.

If the Eagle [U.S.A.] should fail to give the protection that is needed, then the Bear's [Russia's] claws shall tighten upon the Earth. But as the Eagle and the Bear should come, therefore, into clutches, one into the other, the Dragon [China] should come forth and bare forth its teeth. And the whole Earth should smolder, therefore, unto the same.

And therefore, the Seventh Seal will have been opened.

Yet, your Earth shall not perish, nor shall man, for the Lord's hand shall be placed upon the Earth, and the Earth shall change form. And the men with the spiritual development and the women with the spiritual development shall, therefore, come forth and rebuild your earth.

And those from your other galaxies shall, therefore, find that the earth karma of war has ended, and therefore, join them in the rebuilding of this small speck of dust you call Earth.

And a place that our Father may lay His head shall, therefore, come in reality.

These things that were written, these visions that we have implanted upon the Earth, this Seventh Seal does not have to be opened in this manner. The battle of Armageddon, as we have said, may be avoided, if the Eagle [U.S.A.] acts in a valid manner. If he shows weakness, then the Eagle's feathers shall be plucked, and he shall fall from the Heavens. And the war of Armageddon shall be diverted unto the year of 1985. [See *Mark* 13:32.]

Yet, all of these things that we have shown you can be avoided. But only you, as the people of the Earth, can change your paths. We are not allowed to interfere. We are not allowed to take from you the gift of God of free choice. Act, therefore, according to that hidden place of God within you....

Tel Meggido in Israel

You have other questions, ask.

"[11-2-73-005] asks, 'Am I doing what I should be doing with my life, vocational and personal life?'

Yes, we see thy need, and we shall answer in this manner. Your direction has been good. But we should answer further in this manner. As we have said before, we arc here but for one purpose. That in itself is for the preparation of the coming of the Messiah.

In the beginning of our coming, we did say unto these words — form, therefore, a group. Call of thyselves unto the Spiritual Philosophy of God. Form not unto thee a church, for the church of God should dwelleth in man. Take no man from his religion, but replace that which he has lost and send him back unto his churches. Bring forth, therefore, philosophy and knowledge.

And this we should say unto you. For the way to be prepared, it should take of many hands, hands that are willing to work, hands that are willing to carry a yoke of love unto other of mankind.

We did not promise an easy way. We said only that we would provide for the needs of those who were willing to work — not the wants.

We also said that we would provide for the material things that were needed to carry on this work, but not the wants.

And, take from the philosophy that we have given; study it.

Find, therefore, unto thyself that of wisdom or that of false. But seek and you shall receive. Open the door and we shall enter, for we shall provide the bread and the wine if you shall provide the yeast.

November 2, 1973: You have other questions, ask.

"Yes, Aka.[11-2-73-002] asks for a health reading and for spiritual guidance. She wants more spiritual improvement.."

Yes, we see thy need, and first we should answer in this manner.

Of the spiritual development within the same, come there forth and seek from within the group thy belong those who dwell near thee. This would greatly help in your development. We have provided the philosophy, yet there are many others.

We do not say unto thee, leave of thy churches. We do not say of thee, cast aside thy faith —

only that thy should come in preparation, as we have come, for we have come for but one purpose, that in itself is the preparation for the coming of the Messiah.

Bring forth this as intended, and thy cup should runneth over, for God dwells within all mankind. All thy must do is open the door that we may enter.

November 9, 1973: And for those who are wise and shall listen, they shall hear.

And for those who wish to see may see even though they are blinded, for the light is placed before all.

We have placed, as we promised, unto the heavens that that each of you shall share, each in your own way, yet each of you shall know of our presence.

And we shall reach upon the Earth, a third of the Earth at a time, yet all of the Earth shall know of our presence. But yet, there will be some who cannot see, and they shall not look.

There will be some who will say, "This is a natural phenomena."

And we say unto you, not one speck of dust upon your Earth could not be moved without our Father's permission, for He who created all things, both upon Heaven and Earth, has placed, therefore, a promise, and He has not failed to give you, each of you, a sign in your own way.

Continue to look into the heavens, but also look upon the Earth in your day-to-day toil at the many miracles, as you would call them, that God performs for you every day.

Place, therefore, within yourself once a day that small time of thanksgiving. Take out that moment within your day to give thanks unto the Lord for your many blessings.

Count them before you start your day, and your faith shall grow and multiply.

November 18, 1973: You have other questions, ask.

"Yes, Aka. He asks for the causes for mental and physical grief and instability of last year and asks how this fits in with spiritual development, and how can he gain calm and vital energy?"

First, we should answer in this manner. Once the physical problem has been taken from this subject, the mental and spiritual growth shall begin within the same.

You speak of your problems of last year, yet we shall say unto you, look back unto where you have been. This within itself shall fit within the parable of the porpoise. Study this well, for upon this Earth each soul seeks out its own karmic action.

But should you go before and lay yourself before a butcher, and a butcher shall take you and butcher you. Should you lay yourself into the flowers, then harmony shall grow with the same. But should you say unto yourself, "I shall take only the flowers of the earth," then a disharmony should grow.

That that thy seek out, thy find in this Earth form, for this is a learning time. If it is a time that you would experiment with and learn and place into practice that that you have known before, for remember, you are all parts of that that you have been before. Taking these things into consideration, that that you give shall be returned to you in kind, in all manners, for is it not written that, "he who should slay with the sword shall be slain with the sword."

But there is a time for the picking up of a sword to defend thyself. This is not against God's commandments.

It is said, "Thy shall not kill." But it is also said, stand firm upon thy beliefs unless proven wrong. Protect of thy kind, but do so in a just and righteous manner, killing not for the sake of killing, but killing knowing you detest that which you have to do. Yet do nothing unto one another that you would not, placed in the same situation, wish to be done back unto yourself. For remember,

the Lord giveth and the Lord taketh away. Yet the Lord taketh nothing He does not replace tenfold.

We have come but for one purpose. Our purpose is the preparation for the coming of the Messiah.

Our Lord spoke unto us before, and yet again, "FOR THESE OF MY CHILDREN ARE A STUBBORN LOT, AND THEY LEARN VERY SLOWLY. BEAR WITH THEM." He said unto us, "FOR THERE IS MANY THINGS YOU MUST TELL THEM OVER AND OVER."

And so we say unto you, we place forth from this day forward the wine and the bread, that you supply of the yeast.

Open the door that we may enter, and the growth thy ask for shall be placed within thy grasping hands.

But do not grasp it. Let it flow within you as a free, beautiful thing, as a rose without thorns, and all beauty shall come forth in full blossom.

November 23, 1973: Yes, we see thy need, and we should answer in this manner.

For those who have ears, let them listen; for those who are deaf, let them listen. For those who are blind, let them listen. Yet for those who have sight, let them see.

For upon your land, as we have said before, marches onward unto the Fifth Angel.

We have told unto thee of the coming of the famine, and yet your nation, your world did nothing. We also told you that this need not be.

Yet we should tell unto you

the parable of the tree, the woodsman and the young boy.

For as the woodsman and the young boy went into the forest and cut, therefore, a huge tree, and the woodsman was busy cutting away the branches and leaves of the tree, the young boy called unto him and said unto him these words, "Sir, what does all the circles in the trunk of the tree mean?"

And the woodsman answered back, and he said unto them, "If the circles are thin, those are dry and hard years for the tree in its growth. If they are fat, then those were plentiful years for the tree. Yet each circle should constitute a lifetime of the tree within the same, for all should come from the heart of the tree."

The lad looked long at the circles. He said, "Yes, but sir, there are circles that lead back into one part of another circle."

The woodsman stopped his work and ventured forward, and therefore, looked unto the trunk of the tree as the lad would. And he shook his head and could not understand this. And he told unto the lad, "I do not understand this, but maybe God would. Let us give prayer unto God that He should answer our question."

And as they bent their head in prayer a stranger approached, and as both the boy and the woodsman looked up they were surprised. The stranger walked forward and laid his hand unto the tree trunk and he said, "Look, therefore, unto the heart of the tree. In the beginning, it was pure and clean. Yet you see, therefore, of the days of famine for the tree; yet it grew and grew in knowledge. Yet there were days when it received plenty of nourishment, and those are the wider circles. Yet you see, even the wider circle comes back unto one of the thinner circles.

"And I say unto you into these words, for the tree had its own karma and learned not from it. A stone was cast there by a thoughtless person, and the tree, knowing not how to rid itself of it, the circles led back into the same place. But yet, you see beyond this, and the circles once again become even and whole, for the tree, like man, took many lifetimes to learn to cast out its karma, its problem."

And we say unto you that even though the back of the tree has been blemished, if that which is inside of the tree in the beginning stands forth unto all stones that are cast upon it, the bark shall return and the tree shall grow forth. And this is much as the same as a man, for the body of man is the temple of God. Man may cast stones and harm the bark, but it cannot destroy that which is truthfully inside. That is the soul and the spirit which is enhoused within the body, the temple of God.

Yet we say unto you, destroy this temple, and if that which came from the inside was pure, it shall restore itself in three days.

Before you stands that which you would say is the birth of the one known
as Jesus Christ.

He said unto you unto these words, "I come of this time, not to bring peace upon the earth, but to show you the fulfillment of the prophecies yet to come." And so he did. And he showed unto you the resurrection of the body in three day, yet you knew him not.

And yet we come but for one purpose, to prepare the way for his coming, the coming of the Messiah. And yet his name should not be Jesus, or Mohammed, or Buddha; for the name shall come from our Father, and the spirit shall come from our Father.

Yet before you lies this land of Israel. And our Father promised that they should return unto their land. And our Father promised that the Lamb that you had slain should come forth.

But He has also said unto you, beware of the anti-Christ which come upon your earth, for it shall be a beast, and even though its head shall be cut away, a new head shall come forth from it, for she is a foul thing, this nation of Babylon.

We have told unto you that that of your Book of Revelations should now have its second fulfillment, for you shall be as those of the modern Romans.

Yet we have told unto you that the children of God may be changed as though the picking up of a stone. But this must come from within.

Yet all parts, as the tree has done, must repair itself, and prepare itself in a like manner. We have said unto thee, if thy eye offend thee, cast it aside. The tree did not kill itself by casting aside the stone. It repaired that within itself and went on with life. Do so within yourselves.

December 7, 1973:

For from the heavens thy shall find within your Book is written that the stars shall fall from the heavens, and the earth shall be cleansed, and a new Messiah shall be born upon your earth.

[See *The Revelation*, chapter 12.]

Soon you shall celebrate the birth of the one known as Jesus Christ.

He said unto those who would listen, "Look unto the heavens, and ye shall know that I shall return upon the earth. Therefore, be good shepherds unto your flocks and tend my fields." [See *Acts* 1:6–11 and *John* 21:15–17.]

We are here but for one purpose, that is the preparation for the coming of the Messiah.

The Fifth Angel walks upon your earth. None further need walk. Now is the time of the Cherub.

December 28, 1973: We shall leave with this message.

Your new Messiah now dwells upon your earth in child form. He shall be protected.

Glory be the name of the Lord.

Please continue reading — See part 2 of 3 of "The Preparation for the coming of the Messiah" (the 1974 to 1977 messages). Then read part 3 of 3 (the 1978 to 1989 messages on the "coming of the Messiah."

The Preparation for the Coming of the Messiah

Part 2 of 3: The messages spoken on the coming of the Messiah by the spiritual messengers of God, Aka, from 1974 through 1977

The Preparation for the Coming of the Messiah

Part 3 of 3: The messages spoken on the coming of the Messiah by the spiritual messengers of God, Aka, from 1978 through 1989

In *Prepare for the Time of the Great Famine*

"For the valley has been laid before you"

We should say unto those who seek to prepare a place for the people,

A brilliant light passed over Earth, March 25, 1970; it shone in the east through April for all to see. With it spiritual messengers of God arrived and began to speak through an unconscious man in a town named Globe to the world. They "were sent for the one who asked our Father."

Join with the spiritual messengers of God, Aka, in the Association of Universal Philosophy they asked us to form

Become a subscribing member or donate

Go to *https://aup589.wixsite.com/joinaup* on the internet

Email *AUP@erthlink.net*

Or write to

The Association of Universal Philosophy, Inc.

4543 E. Dripping Springs Road

Winkelman, AZ 85192

Please join us!

Read more of the words of the spiritual messengers of God on Amazon.com in their books and e-books.

Search for Aka, spiritual messengers of God on Amazon. Or go to their author page by clicking the link to Aka, spiritual messengers of God, under Follow the author. Then see About the Author and their many books.

You can also read their articles on many topics on the internet. See Medium.com at A Stairway to Heaven – https://medium.com/a-stairway-to-heaven.

Click "What do spiritual messengers of God say to us?" under the main picture at the top.

You can also click on "Rays of Philosophy" to see the newsletters members receive when they join the Association as subscribing members.

Or scroll down to see many of the angels' articles.

May you be blessed.

Made in the USA
Las Vegas, NV
02 January 2025

13548329R10155